STRIKES, PICKETING AND INSIDE CAMPAIGNS

A Legal Guide for Unions

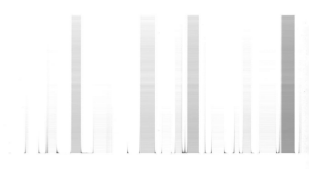

ROBERT M. SCHWARTZ

STRIKES, PICKETING AND INSIDE CAMPAIGNS

A LEGAL GUIDE FOR UNIONS

DRAWINGS BY NICK THORKELSON

Work Rights Press

work rights press

Cambridge, Massachusetts

ISBN 978-0-945902-15-7

Library of Congress Control Number: 2005902298

Work Rights Press
Box 391066
Cambridge, Massachusetts 02139
Telephone: 1-800-576-4552

Also available from Work Rights Press: *The Legal Rights of Union Stewards, How to Win Past Practice Grievances,* and *The FMLA Handbook,* all by Robert M. Schwartz. (See order form on page 165.)

Experienced unions know that the threat of a strike is their most effective bargaining device.

—Employer's Guide to Strike Planning and Prevention

[The strike] is an economic weapon which in great measure implements and supports the principles of the collective bargaining system.

—NLRB v. Erie Resistor Corp. (U.S. Supreme Court)

As we enter our third month of a strike against Vons and Pavilions and a lockout imposed by Ralphs and Albertsons, it is obvious that we are up against a pack of brutal, arrogant, and heartless wolves in the corporate world.

—UFCW Local 4

We have petitioned, we have remonstrated, we have supplicated, we have prostrated ourselves at the foot of the throne, but it has been all in vain. We must fight! - I repeat it sir, we must fight.

—Patrick Henry, American revolutionary

Contents

Author's Note

This book is for trade unionists whose contracts are running out or who are seeking a first agreement. In most contract drives the union achieves a settlement through the push and pull of negotiations. But if the employer is intransigent, or intent on driving down standards, the union must be prepared to flex its muscles.

Waging a successful inside campaign or a full-scale strike demands bold leaders, courageous members, labor allies, and community support. Sad to say, avoiding the pernicious trip-wires in the National Labor Relations Act (NLRA) is also a necessity. Without a basic understanding of lal or law a union risks prosecution, lawsuits, discharges, even de-unionization.

It was not supposed to be this way. Congress enacted the NLRA during the Great Depression so that workers could organize without fear of employer repression. Section 7 declared that employees have the right to take part in union and collective activities. Section 8 forbade discrimination. Section 13 certified the right to strike.

It was not long, however, before Congress and the courts retreated from these guarantees. The first blow came in 1938, when the Supreme Court legalized the hiring of nonunion replacements to permanently replace strikers. The Taft–Hartley Act of 1947 amended the NLRA to allow unions to be prosecuted and sued for a myriad of activities, including interference with strikebreakers and secondary strikes. The Landrum–Griffin Act of 1959 further restricted union picketing. The assault continued in 1984, when the National Labor Relations Board (NLRB), the agency charged with enforcing the NLRA, issued a code of conduct for strikes that a union of nuns would have trouble observing.

This is not to say that victories have become impossible. As Steve Early's foreword argues, the current refrain that "the strike is dead" is as much wishful thinking as a fact on the ground. Truckers, nurses, university workers, and others have shown that winning a strike is not out of reach.

There was a time when the militancy of American trade unions inspired workers around the world; no other labor movement engaged in strikes more frequently or more effectively. *Strikes, Picketing and Inside Campaigns* is for those who want to breathe new life into this legacy.

Dare to struggle, dare to win.

The author can be reached at robertmschwartz@comcast.net

Acknowledgments

Many trade unionists and labor lawyers offered their insight and advice as I struggled to boil down the mass of strike-related legal minutiae. I thank them heartily.

Unionists include Jeff Bolen (UFCW), David Cohen (UE), Edward Collins (IBEW), Richard de Vries (IBT), Steve Early (CWA), Frank Hallstead (IBT), Paul Hannon (USWA), Peter Knowlton (UE), Tom Leedham (IBT), John Murphy (IBT), Richard O'Flaherty (ATU), Rand Wilson (CWA), and Ellen Wallace (UAW).

Lawyers included Ellis Boal, Bryan Decker, Bruce Feldacher, Julius Getman, Polly Halfkenny, Aaron Krakow, Gay Semel, Alan Shapiro, and Christopher Souris.

Naturally, I am solely responsible for any errors or deficiencies.

Caveat Emptor

L abor law in the United States is known for its pendulum-like swings: decades-old policies often change dramatically when a president takes office and appoints new members of the National Labor Relations Board and a new General Counsel. The Republican victory in the 2004 elections insures that the Board will continue its recent pattern of tightening restrictions on unions while relaxing those on employers. Unions should consult their legal counsels in case a rule described in this book is eliminated or modified.

Strikes, Picketing and Inside Campaigns is based on the National Labor Relations Act (NLRA). The NLRA covers private sector employers and employees with the notable exceptions of rail and air carriers and agricultural laborers. Unions in these industries and occupations, as well as unions in the government sector, must look elsewhere for guidance.[1]

Finally: as the focus of this book is contract campaigns, it does not discuss area standards or recognitional picketing, techniques that are primarily associated with organizing.

Foreword

by Steve Early
International Representative, Communications Workers of America

I n the fall of 2002, the streets of Boston, Massachusetts were filled with inspiring scenes of immigrant worker activism during an unprecedented strike by local janitors. Their walkout was backed by other union members, community activists, students and professors, public officials, religious leaders, and even a few "socially-minded" businessmen. The janitors had long been invisible, mistreated by management and, until recently, ignored by their own local union. By making their strike such a popular social cause they achieved what many regarded as a major victory.

The same day that the janitors' dispute was settled a much larger strike at Overnite Transportation ended quite differently. Faced with mounting legal setbacks and dwindling picket line support, the Teamsters were forced to call off their nationwide walkout against the nation's leading nonunion trucker. Four thousand Overnite workers were not able to win a first contract. Since their three-year long strike was suspended, most have lost their bargaining rights in a series of decertification elections.

The intersecting trajectory of these two struggles — one hopeful, the other tragic — raises important questions about the future of unions in America.

Strike activity in the United States has become a high-stakes venture, involving considerable legal and financial risks. As the number of walkouts has declined, the pool of union members and leaders with direct strike experience has begun to shrink as well. Nevertheless, maintaining strike capacity, the ability to walk out and win, is a crucial part of revitalizing and restructuring our unions. Although widely neglected, this task is just as important as shifting greater resources into organizing or political action.

Collectively and individually, unions need to analyze their strike victories and defeats so the lessons of these battles become the basis for future success, not a reoccurring pattern of failure. We must also build stronger community-labor support for strikes so that no group of workers, on any picket line, ends up isolated, impoverished, or alone.

Labor's organizational strength and strike effectiveness have long been connected. Throughout history, work stoppages have been used to alter the balance of power between labor and capital within single workplaces, whole industries, or entire nations. Strikes have won shorter hours and safer conditions through legislation or contract negotiation. They have fostered new forms of worker organization like industrial unions. Strikes have acted as incubators for class-consciousness, rank-and-file leadership, and political activism. In some countries, strikes have challenged and changed dictatorial and oppressive governments.

In Korea, South Africa, France, and Spain, where strikes helped democratize society, general strikes are still used for mass mobilization and protest. In recent years millions of Italians have taken part in nationwide work stoppages directed at budget cuts and changes in labor law. In Brazil, voters have even chosen one-time strike leader Luiz Inacio "Lula" da Silva to be president of their country.

Unfortunately, in the United States major work stoppages have become a statistical blip on the radar screen of industrial relations. Since 1995, walkouts affecting 1,000 or more workers have averaged less than 30 a year. In 2004 there were only 17, with just 316,000 union workers participating. In contrast, in 1952, the peak of labor's post-World War II strike wave, there were 470 major strikes involving nearly three million workers nationwide.

Beginning with the PATCO disaster in 1981, when thousands of striking air traffic controllers were fired and replaced, the U.S. labor movement entered a dark decade of lost strikes and lockouts. Anti-concession battles ended badly at Phelps-Dodge, Greyhound, Hormel, Eastern, Continental Airlines, International Paper, and other firms. Lost strikes discouraged other unions from using labor's traditional weapon. Among those that did, setbacks continued into the mid-'90s at firms like Caterpillar, Bridgestone/Firestone, and A. E. Staley.

Even during this difficult period for strikers, there were union struggles that bucked the tide of concession bargaining. In 1989, for example, 60,000 members of the Communications Workers of America and the International Brotherhood of Electrical Workers waged an effective four-month strike in New York and New England over threatened medical benefit cuts at NYNEX. The telephone workers used ambulatory picketing tactics like those recommended in *Strikes, Picketing and Inside Campaigns*, and targeted top company officials and their allies in places where they least expected it. (See Chapter 6, "Making It Personal.")

In the Appalachian coalfields that same year, the United Mine Workers succeeded in making their 12-month walkout against Pittston a national labor cause. The union mobilized its members for sympathy strikes at other companies, linked arms with Jesse Jackson, used civil disobedience tactics, staged the first plant occupation since the 1930s, and created "Camp Solidarity" to host strike supporters from around the country. Even an avalanche of injunctions, fines, and damage suits did not deter the miners and their families.

Just a few years later, West Virginia aluminum workers, locked out by Ravenswood, applied many lessons of the Pittston strike in a wide-ranging corporate campaign by the United Steel Workers of America. The USWA leveraged international union connections to put pressure on key financial institutions and investors tied to the employer. (See Chapter 5 "Extending the Strike" via "Foreign Connections.") Despite massive hiring of replacement workers and other union-busting measures, Ravenswood was finally forced to end its lockout and settle with the USWA. Since that victory, west coast dockworkers and Bay Area hotel workers have both turned the table on offensive employer lockouts.

In 1997, the strike made its biggest comeback in recent years with a nationwide walkout by 190,000 United Parcel Service workers. Support from Teamster drivers has long been appreciated by other strikers. As *Strikes, Picketing and Inside Campaigns* notes in Chapter 9, "Honor Thy Line," IBT contract language has been "a boon for unions that want Teamster drivers to respect their picket lines." In 1997 it was time for the rest of labor to return the favor, which unions did in a tremendous outpouring of support for UPS drivers and package handlers.

The way the Teamsters framed their dispute with UPS was critical in gaining public sympathy. The main strike objective was to create more full-time jobs, to thwart management's strategy of converting UPS into a largely part-time workforce. "Part-Time America Doesn't Work!" the Teamsters proclaimed, successfully investing their contract fight with larger social meaning. The UPS strike not only beat back the company's concession demands and made job security gains. It became a rallying point for everyone concerned about part timing and its accompanying erosion of job-based benefits.

Unions struggling against health care cost shifting have borrowed from the Teamsters' playbook in linking their strikes to the movement for health care reform. When 18,000 General Electric workers staged a two-day nationwide walkout to protest medical plan changes, many organized around the slogan, "Health Care For All, Not Health Cuts at GE!" Strike-related rallies and publicity emphasized the common bond between union and nonunion, insured and uninsured workers.

Union members are now striking with greater tactical flexibility than before, experimenting with intermittent walkouts and inside campaigns to reduce the risk and cost of protracted shutdowns. In the auto industry, unions have exploited new strike vulnerability arising from management's reliance on "just-in-time" parts delivery to auto assembly plants. UAW walkouts at Johnson Controls, a parts supplier for Ford and DaimlerChrysler, won first contracts and neutrality agreements through indirect pressure on their customers.

At Yale, members of separate white-collar and blue-collar bargaining units repeatedly showed solidarity in campus-based organizing and bargaining. In 2003, these Hotel and Restaurant locals skirmished creatively with the university for the ninth time in 35 years. In the wake of aggressive picketing, mass rallies, and strike-related arrests, Yale sued for peace with a long-term contract settlement.

In similar fashion, thousands of telephone workers in the northeast entered bargaining with Verizon in 2003 with a record of five strikes in the previous 20 years, and a deeply ingrained "no contract, no work" tradition. Confronted with unprecedented strike contingency plans by management, members of CWA and IBEW shifted gears to throw their corporate adversary off balance. For more than a month they worked without a contract, engaging in job wobbling activities as described in Chapter 2. Verizon incurred enormous strike-preparation costs but never had a chance to replace its workforce with an army of scabs. The result was a new contract that preserved job security guarantees and full medical coverage for workers and retirees.

The experience at Verizon, like others cited above, shows that worker militancy can take many different forms and still be effective. The key to success, whether on strike or in pursuing a non-strike strategy, is creativity, careful planning, and membership involvement. *Strikes, Picketing and Inside Campaigns* can help by laying out the full range of legal options, allowing unions to evaluate the pros and cons of different courses of action.

For the employer, one key tactic of intimidation is the deployment of legal counsel, whose job is to turn collective bargaining into a legal morass in which union members' concerns eventually get lost. In this invaluable guide, Bob Schwartz helps to even the scales on the legal front. *Strikes, Picketing and Inside Campaigns* gives us a unique tool to use in membership education and leadership training, rank-and-file debate, and strategy discussion of what to do and how to do it when a contract expires. Any union members who fail to consult Schwartz before "taking on the boss" will not be as ready as they could be. Any union negotiator who doesn't have this book will miss information and advice that could make the hard job of getting a good contract just a little bit easier.

Chapter 1

Setting the Table

Preconditions • Renegotiation notice • Dispute notice

I t may sound surreal, but an innocent failure to send a one-sentence notice to an obscure government agency can jeopardize the jobs of every employee in the bargaining unit. The reason: legal preconditions to the right to strike.

Preconditions

Section 8(d) of the National Labor Relations Act (NLRA) levies three requirements on a union seeking a successor collective bargaining agreement:

1. At least 60 days before the current contract expires (90 days for health care unions), the union must inform management in writing that it intends to terminate or modify the agreement and is willing to meet and confer on a new one. The union may not strike between the date it gives notice and the date the contract expires.

2. Within 30 days of notice to the employer (60 days for health care unions), the union must notify the Federal Mediation and Conciliation Service (FMCS) that a labor dispute is in progress.

3. Simultaneously with notice to the FMCS, the union must serve a similar notice on a labor mediation agency established by a state or territory where the dispute is located.

If the union does not satisfy each of these obligations it cannot walk out when the contract expires. If it strikes, the employer can dismiss the participants, even if the reason for the union's breach is a clerical error.[2]

Renegotiation notice

A union can mail, fax or hand deliver the 60-day renegotiation notice. The most secure method is certified mail, return receipt requested. The union can compose its own notice or use an FMCS F-7 form (available on the FMCS website: *www.fmcs.gov*).

Calculating the final day. To calculate the last day to serve your employer, take the collective bargaining agreement's expiration date as day one and count back to 60.

Example: Local 100's contract with Rich Foods expires on October 15, 2006. On or before August 17, 2006, the union must deliver a notice similar to the following:

"Local 100 gives notice to Rich Foods for the purpose of terminating the current agreement and entering into negotiations for a new one."

Note: Some contracts require that the union serve a renegotiation notice 90 days prior to expiration.

Modify or terminate? Generally, it does not matter whether a union uses the words "modify" or "terminate" to indicate its bargaining intentions. However, if the current agreement provides that a notice to modify extends the contract, only a termination notice will preserve the union's right to strike.

Dispute notice

Section 8(d) appears to allow telephone or face-to-face notice to the mediation agencies. Nevertheless, the safest and most secure method is certified mail, return receipt requested. Most unions mail F-7s to the employer and the mediation services on the same day.

Addresses. The FMCS headquarters is 2100 K Street N.W., Washington, D.C. 20427. Regional FMCS offices are located in 80 cities. State and territorial mediation agencies are listed on the website of the Association of Labor Relations Agencies (*www.alra.org*). If a state is not listed, send your notice to the state department of labor or labor board. Some states do not offer mediation services. In that case, local notice is not required.[3]

Late notice. A union that serves its employer after the 60-day mark may still conduct a protected strike (assuming the delay did not trigger an automatic renewal clause), but it must wait 60 days from the service date. Similarly, if the union is late in serving the FMCS, the state mediation agency, or both, it can strike 30 days after furnishing the required notices.[4]

Example: Local 3, representing newspaper workers in Michigan, served a termination notice 90 days before the contract's expiration date and sent a copy to the FMCS. Negotiations with the employer were unsuccessful and the union prepared to strike. One day before expiration, the union realized that it had failed to give notice to the Michigan Bureau of Employment Relations. Instead of risking an unprotected strike, the union delivered a dispute notice to the state agency and waited 30 days before walking out.

Employer gives notice. An employer anxious for contract concessions may initiate a termination notice. In that event, the employer must notify the federal and state mediation services. If it doesn't, it cannot implement a final proposal or declare a lockout—even if negotiations with the union come to an impasse.[5]

FIRST CONTRACT

Q. We are negotiating our first contract. Do we have to notify the FMCS before calling a strike?

A. No. Except in the health care industry, Section 8(d)'s notice requirements only apply to second or later contracts. In health care, a union negotiating its first contract must notify the FMCS 30 days before serving a strike notice.[6]

QUICK RETREAT

Q. On the third day of our walkout, the general manager told us that the state mediation service has no record of receiving the union's F-7 form. He says this makes the strike illegal and he will fire everyone if we don't return by tomorrow. What should we do?

A. You are safe if you have a certified mail receipt from the agency. Otherwise you are in trouble and should go back to work.

CHESS MOVE

Q. Is my reading of Section 8(d) correct, that if we send a termination notice but refrain from notifying the mediation services, we can prevent the employer from imposing new terms or locking us out when the contract expires?

A. No. The party that issues the 60-day termination notice is the only one with an obligation to inform the mediation agencies.

OVERTIME CAMPAIGN

Q. We forgot to serve notices on the mediation agencies before the contract expired and are waiting 30 days to strike. In the meantime, can we refuse overtime?

A. No. The NLRA defines a strike as a concerted stoppage of work, slowdown, or other interruption of operations.[7]

Chapter 2

No Contract – No Peace

Inside campaigns • Work without a contract—what's in
jeopardy? • Death by 1000 cuts

As the last minutes of a contract tick down with no agreement in
sight, the union must consider its options. One is to strike. A
second is to temporarily extend the contract while carrying out
elements of an inside campaign. A third is to let the contract expire, work
day-by-day, and conduct a full-fledged inside campaign.

Inside campaigns

Inside campaigns have several things to recommend them. For one, "job-
wobbling" activities such as handbills, rallies, off-duty picketing, overtime
refusals, work-to-rule, and grievance walkouts, along with the threat of
full-scale strike, may create enough pressure that the employer agrees to

settle the contract. For another,
the employer may respond in
ways that violate the National
Labor Relations Act (NLRA).
It may videotape workers as
they handbill or rally. It may
prohibit employees from meeting in the lunchroom. It may

WORK TO RULE

warn workers that they face discharge if they take part in picketing or consumer boycott activities. ULPs of this nature give the union an opportunity to call an unfair-labor-practice strike, a walkout in which employees are
protected against permanent replacement. (See Chapters 13 and 14.)

An inside campaign may provoke the employer into initiating a lockout.
It might sound illogical, but if you are going to hit the bricks anyhow, a
lockout has advantages over a strike. The public and other unions will be
more responsive to solidarity requests. Thirty-four states and Puerto Rico
pay unemployment insurance to locked out workers (see list on page 92).
The employer will be barred from hiring permanent replacements. Finally,
running a "clean" lockout is not easy: if the employer violates a labor law
rule (see Chapter 15), the NLRB may declare the lockout unlawful and
order workers reinstated with full back pay.

Work without a contract—what's in jeopardy?

A common fear about letting the contract expire is that the employer can
cut wages, halt payments to benefit plans, cancel vacations, scrap seniority, assign supervisors to unit work, refuse to hear grievances, and so on.

In truth, the NLRA requires management to maintain contract terms and
conditions of employment while it bargains on a new agreement, except for
the matters discussed below.[8] Abandoning or changing a pre-existing condition is an unfair labor practice (ULP), giving the union a basis for filing an
NLRB charge, calling a ULP strike, or filing a challenge to a lockout.

Areas in jeopardy are union security, dues checkoff, agreements on permissive subjects, arbitration, and matters in the employer's final contract offer.

Union security and dues checkoff. Union-security obligations — the duty to join the union within 30 or 60 days of hire — are unenforceable in the absence of an executed contract. Dues checkoff is also at risk: unless language in the expired agreement provides for the procedure to continue indefinitely, the employer can stop making deductions.[9] Members will still owe dues, but the union will have to collect individually.

Arbitration. With three exceptions, the arbitration duty generally disappears during the without-a-contract period. The exceptions are: grievances filed while the contract was still in effect; grievances over events that occurred prior to expiration; and grievances over rights that accrued under the expired agreement. For grievances over new matters, including discharges, the employer's only duty is to discuss the matter with the union and to supply information.

With arbitration no longer a concern, the employer may be tempted to fire workers who play leading role in inside campaign activities. A counterweight is the union's ability to strike in protest (the no-strike/no lockout clause expires with the contract). The union can also file charges at the NLRB, which, without a contract in force, will not apply its deferral policy.[10]

Agreements on permissive subjects. Contract termination releases the employer from agreements covering permissive subjects of bargaining. Health insurance for already retired employees is one example. Neutrality accords and promises not to relocate are also at risk.

Final proposals. A last area of jeopardy is the employer's final contract offer. Under NLRA rules, if the union and the employer come to a deadlock in contract negotiations, and the preceding contract has expired, the employer can declare impasse and implement its proposals. While the union cannot ignore this possibility, several obstacles stand in the employer's way:

• The employer may not implement a change unless the parties have reached a bargaining impasse on the contract as a whole: Impasse on a single proposal is not sufficient.[11]

- The employer may not declare impasse if the union is in the process of making counteroffers; the employer has insisted on permissive bargaining subjects; the employer has committed ULPs that have contributed to the deadlock; union information requests are pending on disputed proposals; or the employer has otherwise failed to bargain with the union in good faith.

- The employer may not implement a proposal on a partial basis. For example, if its health insurance proposal has four parts, it must implement each. Nor may the employer impose a change that is stricter or more disadvantageous than in a proposal presented to the union during negotiations. The employer can, however, pick and choose among entire proposals.

- The employer may not implement a proposal that deprives employees of an NLRA right, such as the right to strike, to picket, to distribute literature, or to bargain on future changes.

- The employer must continue to observe unaffected terms in the expired collective bargaining agreement.

Note: Angered by an inside campaign, an employer may consider adding harsh proposals to its bargaining demands so that it can retaliate against the union upon reaching an impasse. The Board has ruled, however, that the submission of new demands at late stages of negotiations, especially when they void previously accepted items or revive proposals that were previously abandoned, is bad-faith bargaining and precludes the employer from declaring a lawful impasse.[12]

Death by 1000 cuts

The most successful inside campaigns employ a constellation of activities to increase tension and disrupt the employer. As explained by one organizer:

> The key is that you create a situation so that management, from the time they get up in the morning till the time they go to bed, they worry about what you're doing. And if you're doing a good job, they wake up with nightmares.

Many innovative inside campaign techniques are described in the popular guide *A Troublemakers Handbook 2*.[13] This section discusses tactics whose legality has been litigated at the NLRB.

Note: Two inside campaign pitfalls are partial and intermittent strikes. A partial strike occurs when workers slow production or refuse to perform expected tasks. Examples: instructors who refuse to turn in grades; nurses who refuse to work mandatory overtime. An intermittent strike is a series of work stoppages intended to harass the employer into a state of confusion. Labor law does not protect partial or intermittent strikes— even if the contract has expired. The employer may fire employees who take part.

Handbills. Handbills and newsletters build unity and rankle management. Handbills can express strong opinions, including accusations of mismanagement and strong-arm tactics.[14] The employer may not station managers or supervisors in close proximity in order to surveil the activity.[15]

Unless it disrupts operations, an employer must allow handbilling before and after work and during breaks on outside areas such as parking lots, walkways, and steps.[16] The employer must also permit handbilling in inside non-work or mixed-use areas such as cafeterias and smoking rooms.[17] Management may not confiscate handbills placed on lunch tables prior to employees taking their seats.[18]

At or away from the workplace, workers can handbill customers, the public, and other employees with appeals for support. If the union handbills at the location of another employer, it must avoid picketing or calls for a sympathy strike. It can display a stationary banner.

Rallies. A union can hold contract campaign rallies and informational meetings before work, after work, and during break times. Unless the event interferes with operations or causes disciplinary problems, the employer must permit employees to gather on parking lots and outside walkways.[19] Employer videotaping of peaceful protests is illegal.[20] The union may also hold rallies off premises.

Insignia. Employees can wear contract campaign insignia such as buttons, armbands, shirts, hats, and ribbons. Possible legends: "No contract, no peace," "Fight for a fair contract," "Stop union busting," "Don't touch our health care," "Up your final offer." A solidarity day—for example, everyone wearing red shirts—is protected by the NLRA unless it violates an enforced dress code. Cars may display signs in company parking lots.

An employer can bar a particular button or insignia if it is obscene, incites violence, interferes with safety or quality, disrupts production, creates disciplinary problems, or upsets customers. Management may not act on speculation: it must have evidence that the insignia is having the claimed effect.[21]

An employer may enforce a total ban on insignia if "special circumstances" justify the rule. The NLRB allows hospitals to ban insignia in patient-care areas. Retail stores can do the same on the selling floor. A company whose employees wear uniforms while dealing with the public can also ban insignia.[22]

An employer that bans insignia must enforce its policy consistently and across the board. If a hospital allows nurses to wear religious, holiday, or political buttons, it cannot forbid insignia with contract campaign legends.[23]

Off-duty picketing. One of the most dramatic campaign tactics is off-duty picketing. (If an extended contract forbids picketing, this tactic will have to await expiration.)

Employees have a protected right to picket before and after their shifts and during breaks — even if operations are in progress.[24] Picket signs should refer to the labor dispute. Example: "Fighting for a fair contract. Honk if you're with us."

Although it is not widely appreciated, off-duty pickets have the right to ask customers, contractors, and delivery workers not to cross their picket line.[25] Union drivers whose contracts permit them to respect "primary" picket lines can honor requests.

Off-duty picketing is guaranteed to set management's hair on fire, especially if outside personnel honor the line. Nonetheless, the employer cannot discipline workers for disloyalty, force employees to choose between picketing and working, lay off the individuals involved, or hire replacements.[26]

Unions representing health care employees must give ten days notice to the institution and the FMCS before commencing off-duty picketing.

Work-to-rule. In a work-to-rule activity, also known as work by the book, employees scrupulously follow every order, policy, procedure, or standard issued by management for the performance of their jobs, especially safety and hygiene directives. No one works off the clock, outside his or her job description, or at more than a normal speed. Everyone takes full breaks, and no one volunteers for extra work.

Curiously, the Board has not directly addressed the legal status of work-to-rule or delineated when it crosses the line into unprotected partial strike activity. In one case, however, it allowed workers to stop bringing in personal tools, explaining that, "Where an action is voluntary, the concerted refusal by employees to perform that action is a protected concerted activity and does not con-

stitute an unlawful partial strike."[27]

Employees should not expect NLRA protection if they deliberately reduce their output, refuse assigned duties, stop taking expected shortcuts, or refuse direct orders from management.

Limited-duration strike. A union whose contract has expired can sponsor a limited duration (half-day, full-day, two-day, etc.) strike. The work stoppage can be called over contract demands, a post-expiration grievance, a ULP, or another issue.[28] Health care unions must give ten days advance notice.

Conducting two walkouts during an inside campaign is a risk. Although an argument can be made that an intermittent strike requires three related walkouts,[29] during an open and obvious inside campaign the NLRB may find two stoppages a series or pattern, even if each is called over a different issue.

Note: The intermittent-strike pitfall does not apply to a union that calls a short strike, returns to work, and then strikes indefinitely.[30]

As with an extended strike, a danger exists that the employer will hire permanent replacements. This risk can be reduced by confining the strike to a single day and, soon after it begins, submitting an unconditional offer to come back the next day. A struck employer may not hire permanent replacements after it receives a return-to-work letter.[31]

RETURN-TO-WORK OFFER

(delivered to employer minutes after strike begins)

Date: October 5, 2006
To: Leo Nelson, Production Manager
From: Ken Myers, President, Local 21
Re: Return-to-work offer

Local 21 members struck at 7:00 a.m. today, October 5, 2006, to protest the company's failure to settle the contract.

For each participating employee, and all employees who honor the picket line, the union unconditionally offers to return to work at 7:00 a.m. tomorrow, October 6, 2006.

A union can further reduce the risk of replacement by waiting to strike until the employer commits a ULP, such as a unilateral change or a failure to supply information. Refusing to reinstate employees after a ULP strike violates the NLRA.

An employer may not reprimand, harass, or threaten an employee for taking part in a lawful strike. Nor may it warn that in the future it will hire permanent replacements.[32]

Break-time demonstration. Employees can demonstrate during meal or break periods if they do so without disrupting operations. During lunch, for example, workers might march to the labor relations office to present a petition.[33]

Overtime moratorium. Whether a union can instruct members to refuse overtime depends on whether contract or past practice treats assignments as voluntary. If workers have been free to decline overtime requests without penalty, a union-sponsored moratorium is protected.[34] If overtime is mandatory, repeated refusals are a partial strike.

Customer boycott. To support an inside campaign, employees can urge customers or clients to withhold purchases of the employer's products or services.[35] Unions with boycott restrictions in their bargaining agreements must wait for contract expiration. Possible tactics include:

- Off-duty picketing and handbilling at the workplace
- Handbilling trade shows
- Handbilling customer facilities
- Signs on automobiles
- Airplane banners
- Letters to customers
- Letters to retailers
- Picketing stores that sell the employer's products
- Asking customers to sign no-buy petitions

To ward off charges of disloyalty, handbills and other union literature should refer to the labor dispute and should avoid attacking the quality of the employer's products or services.

CALL-IN RULE

Q. After the contract expired, we held a one-day strike to protest the company's bargaining posture. The next day, management issued each striker a written warning for violating a company rule requiring employees to call in prior to absences. Are the warnings lawful?

A. No. Strikers may not be disciplined for violating call-in or call-out rules.[36]

SICKOUT

Q. Can we call a sickout to support our contract campaign?

A. Yes, if the employer is made aware that the action is being undertaken as a union protest (and the contract has expired).[37]

PENDING CASES

Q. Three grievances are scheduled for arbitration. If we let the contract expire, will they die?

A. No. Unless language in the contract completely extinguishes the arbitration procedure, you will be able to arbitrate pre-expiration grievances. [38]

RETURN AFTER WORK STOPPAGE

Q. The day after the contract expired, we held a morning rally outside the plant gate. At nine o'clock we told the general manager we were ready to work without conditions. His response: "Today is history. See you tomorrow." Should we file a ULP charge?

A. Yes. Absent a substantial business justification, an employer must immediately reinstate workers who offer to return from a lawful work stoppage.[39]

TEMP AGENCY CONTRACT

Q. When we tried to come back from a walkout the boss said we would have to wait because he had signed a five-day contract with a temporary employment agency. Is this lawful?

A. Probably not. A contract with a replacement agency is generally not a sufficient reason to delay strikers from returning.[40]

PICKETING IN UNIFORM

Q. Can we wear uniforms on an off-duty picket line?

A. Perhaps. An employer must tolerate workers picketing in uniform unless, prior to the walkout, it consistently enforced a rule against wearing uniforms off-duty.[41]

TAKING DOWN NAMES

Q. While we handbilled outside the plant, the director of Human Resources wrote our names on a pad of paper. Is this legal?

A. No. Recording or even pretending to record the names of employees who engage in protected activity is illegal.[42] File a ULP charge.

PICKETING BUSINESS

Q. Can we set up a picket line outside a business owned by a company director?

A. No. It is illegal to picket a secondary business (see page 41). But you can handbill or display a stationary banner.

Chapter 3

Hitting the Bricks

Timing • Picket lines • Signs • Conduct • Secondary
picketing • Contractors' gate • Common situs picketing •
Employer ULPs • Court order • Corporate campaign

Before calling a strike, the union should carefully weigh the reasons for and against, including the possibility that the employer will hire permanent replacements. To meet this concern, it may help to jump ahead to Chapter 13, which explains how to position a walkout as an unfair-labor-practice (ULP) strike.

Timing

A union can "hit the bricks" the instant the current agreement expires. Or it can wait until a more favorable juncture, such as a busy day or week, or the start of a new project. Advance notice is only necessary in two circumstances.

Damage to equipment or property. If a walkout is likely to cause cause significant damage to an employer's plant or equipment, or to endanger personnel or customers, the union must take reasonable precautions to prevent harm. This may simply mean shutting down machinery, but bargaining units such as security guards should provide one or two days advance notice.[43]

Health care workers. Section 8(g) of the NLRA compels a health care union to give its employer and the FMCS at least ten days written notice of the date and time of a planned strike, picket, or work refusal.[44] To calculate the last day for the notice, take the day before the strike as day one and count back to ten.

> **Example:** Local 20's contract with Otis Hospital expires at midnight on June 25, 2005. To establish its ability to conduct an immediate strike, the union must deliver notices to the hospital and the FMCS by June 16 along the following lines: "This is to notify you that Local 20 plans to begin a strike and a picket at Otis Hospital at 12:00 a.m. on June 26, 2006."

If a union strikes without giving a required notice, participants can be discharged.[45]

Picket lines

Picket lines publicize the strike and pressure employees, delivery workers, contractors, vendors, and customers not to enter. A union can picket all of the employer's facilities, whether or not they are sites of bargaining unit work. See Chapter 5 for rules about sister branches and divisions.

Location. Both the NLRA and the U.S. Constitution protect labor picketing. Accordingly, unions can patrol on streets, sidewalks, and other public rights-of-way. But because picketing has a confrontational aspect, state and local governments can impose reasonable restrictions on the time, place, and manner.

Restrictions. Most localities forbid pickets from obstructing the free passage of pedestrians and vehicles. Some go further, requiring the union to obtain a permit, insisting that pickets maintain continuous motion, and forbidding profane language. Laws that impose unreasonable restrictions can be challenged on First Amendment grounds.[46]

Driveway entrances. Public rights-of-way usually include strips several feet wide along both sides of the asphalt, which may or may not be covered with sidewalks. If the strip encompasses an intersecting driveway, the apron will be on public property. In these circumstances, the union can picket on the first few feet of the driveway. (See illustration below.) You can check the width of the right-of-way by visiting the public works department and asking for a road layout.

Example: Miller Cosmetics is located on a road that lacks a sidewalk. Miller claims that it owns the entire driveway. But the union obtained a road layout from City Hall that showed that the public right-of-way was 30 feet wide. Since the pavement is only 20 feet wide, it was apparent that land on each side was public property, including the first part of the Miller driveway. (Another possibility was a 10-foot strip on one side, but further checking verified 5-foot strips on each side.)

Violation. An employer commits a ULP if it asks the police to stop the union from picketing on public property or its legal equivalent.[47]

ULP INTERFERENCE CHARGE

1. On June 19, 2005, Local 200 picketed the employer at its Cleveland facility as part of a lawful strike.

2. The union confined its picket line to the public right-of-way.

3. The employer falsely claimed to the police that the pickets were on its property and the police forced the pickets to move.

4. The employer is interfering with activity protected by Section 7 of the NLRA and is prolonging the strike.

Picketing on employer property. If the land underneath a driveway is entirely employer-owned, with no public easement, the union should start the strike by picketing on the driveway. If the police threaten arrests, move the line to the edge of the street or highway. Then file a ULP charge seeking authority to picket on the driveway.

The NLRB can order an employer to permit picketing on its property. One source of authority is *Republic Aviation*, a Supreme Court case that allows workers to engage in concerted activity on employer premises unless the activity disrupts operations or causes disciplinary problems.[48] Another is *Jean Country*, which balances several factors including the hazards of picketing on streets and highways.[49]

ULP ACCESS CHARGE

1. Local 25 is on strike against the employer.

2. On April 10, 2006 the union attempted to picket on the driveway leading to the employer's facility.

3. The employer ordered the pickets off the property and called the police.

4. The union has a Section 7 right to conduct peaceful picketing on outside areas of the employer's property.

5. Picketing on the highway is dangerous and ineffective.

6. The employer is interfering with activity protected by Section 7 of the NLRA and is prolonging the strike.

Police relations. Establishing a relationship with police officials can be helpful if problems arise on the picket line. Prior to the stoppage, visit the police to go over road layouts. If you plan to picket on employer property, ask the police to refrain from making arrests until the NLRB rules on the union's access rights.

If the police threaten to make arrests for interference or blocking, try to agree on a set amount of minutes or seconds before pickets must move aside. Remind the police that under the NLRA, strikers have a protected right to approach line crossers, to ask them not to enter, and to hand out literature, even if this causes momentary traffic interruptions.[50]

If the police impose unreasonable restrictions, speak with the police department's attorney. In an extreme case, the union can threaten a "Golden State" lawsuit, an action against officials for enforcing the law in a way that prevents the union from exerting lawful economic pressure.[51]

Industrial parks. If your employer is located in an industrial park, shopping center, or office building, you may have a right to picket on the property. The NLRB applies a balancing test that considers several factors, including whether the property is open to the public and whether picketing on nearby roads is safe.[52] The Board can order a property owner to allow the union access. In one case it ordered an office building to permit picketing on the 14th floor.[53]

> **Pointer:** Conduct off-duty picketing before the contract expires. If the property owner orders you to leave, file a ULP charge. You may get a settlement or ruling you can use during the strike.

Signs

Unions have considerable latitude when it comes to picket signs, handbills, and other publicity.

"Bloodsucker." Union signs usually refer to the issues in dispute. But nothing prevents a sign from labeling the boss a "union-buster," "bloodsucker," "sweatshop operator," "rat," or "fascist." A striker cannot be punished for expressing an opinion, no matter how imaginative.[54]

Going too far. A boss can sue for defamation if a sign or handbill makes a factual assertion that the union or the picket knows is false. Example: "President Melendez molests children." Courts frequently treat labor dispute accusations as opinions, however, even when they take the form of factual assertions.[55]

Conduct

The union must decide the level of confrontation it wants on the picket line. Pickets have a right to use coarse language and call line crossers scabs. On the other hand, verbal abuse can lead to fights and violence, providing a basis for a judge to issue an injunction against the union.

Hit list. A striker can be disciplined or discharged if he or she:
- Spits on a line crosser
- Places tacks or jack rocks on driveways
- Kicks, scratches, or pounds a car
- Blocks persons or vehicles from entering or leaving
- Throws liquids, eggs, or rocks
- Pursues a vehicle at high speed
- Threatens to harm a delivery driver or other line crosser
- Brandishes a weapon
- Vandalizes the employer's property

See Chapter 12 for more on discharges.

Profanity. Generally speaking, an employer may not take action against a striker for epithets or gestures that do not threaten violence. But discipline may be imposed if sexual, racial, or religious slurs are repeatedly employed against a particular individual.[56] Profanity directed at customers or the public can also lead to punishment.

Disparagement. A striker may criticize the employer and its products in conversations with customers, contractors, and the press.[57] Deliberately spreading falsehoods, such as telling customers that they will die from using a struck product, is not permitted.[58]

Civil disobedience. Nonviolent civil disobedience that does not interfere with persons entering or leaving the struck facility or otherwise disrupt the employer's operations has been found not to be serious misconduct — even when the police make arrests. In 1995, the Detroit News fired 18 strikers because they sat down on newspaper steps after employees had entered for the day and stayed there until they were arrested for trespass. An ALJ overturned the discipline, explaining that:

> The symbolic actions of those who sat down may have been technically illegal . . . but so is parking overtime at a meter, and about as serious.[59]

Secondary picketing

In any strike, it is natural to target businesses that buy from the employer, furnish it with supplies, deliver its products, or help with its financing. The union can impose some pressure by putting the business on an "unfair" list, distributing boycott handbills to customers, and displaying stationary banners (see Chapter 8). But a "secondary boycott" provision in the NLRA forbids picketing or other disruptive activity.

Section 8(b)(4). Section 8(b)(4) of the NLRA, added by the Taft-Hartley Act, prohibits unions from using coercive methods to induce a secondary employer or person to stop doing business with a struck ("primary") employer or to intercede in a labor dispute.[60] Coercion includes picketing, threats to picket, sitting-in, confronting the secondary's employees or customers, and mass rallies.

Activities that have a coercive impact on a secondary are illegal even if the primary purpose of the activity is to put pressure on the struck employer, for example, picketing a hotel while the company president is attending a wedding.

A struck employer or a secondary can file ULP charges against a union that violates Section 8(b)(4). If the NLRB Regional Office issues a complaint, the law requires it to seek a restraining order against the union in federal court. In addition, the struck or the picketed employer can sue for money damages.

Inducing strikes. Section 8(b)(4) also makes it illegal to ask employees of a secondary employer, such as a supplier or customer, to strike or to

PICKET LINE INSTRUCTIONS

To All Pickets

1. The United States Constitution gives you the right to picket your employer and pass out handbills during the strike.

2. Section 7 of the National Labor Relations Act also guarantees your right to picket, handbill, and engage in concerted activity.

3. While picketing you may:

- Ask employees to honor the line, even if they are not members of the bargaining unit.
- Ask persons making deliveries to honor the line.
- Ask customers and the public not to patronize the employer's business.
- Hold up a sign asking motorists to "Honk if you're with us."
- Call strikebreakers scabs.

4. Many federal and state laws impose restrictions on picketing. Assume that the employer will closely monitor your conduct, including videotaping and sound recording. It may also instruct security guards to provoke incidents that it can cite in court. To protect your job and to safeguard the union:

- Cooperate with police officers and obey their instructions. If a problem arises, obtain the officer's name, department affiliation, and badge number. Report the information to your picket captain or the local.
- Picket only where assigned by your picket captain.
- Maintain peaceful and orderly picketing.
- Do not talk to managers, supervisors, line crossers, or strangers who hang around the picket line.
- Picket in single file, keep moving, and maintain adequate space between pickets to allow access through entrances and gates. Should a motor vehicle approach, move out of the way.

- Do not use derogatory language regarding a person's race, ethnic origin, religion, gender, age, or sexual orientation.

- Do not use profanity toward a customer or other member of the public.

- Do not threaten physical harm to a strikebreaker, a customer, or any other person.

- Do not touch or crowd around persons or vehicles approaching or crossing the picket line.

- Do not spit on persons going through the picket line.

- Do not litter.

- Do not bring alcoholic beverages or non-prescription drugs with you to picket duty.

- If the employer establishes a so-called reserved gate for contractors, do not picket the entrance unless authorized by your picket captain.

- Report any incidents involving threatening or dangerous behavior by strikebreakers, supervisors, or guards to your picket captain or the local union. Make note of what happened (date, time, place, descriptions of individuals, witness names).

- Do not interfere with traffic beyond what pedestrians are normally entitled to do. Do not stop in front of a vehicle or walk in front of it more than once. Do not block entrances or exits.

- Do not argue with other pickets. If a problem arises, talk to your picket captain.

- Refer journalists and others with questions to the union's designated spokespersons. Do not answer yourself.

5. If you have questions on how to conduct strike activities, speak with your picket captain or call the local union. Union staff and legal advisors will be available to answer questions and to help maintain an effective picket line.

refuse to use struck products. Sympathy strike requests are forbidden in any form, including letters, leaflets, and personal appeals.

> **Note:** Section 8(b)(4) does not bar pickets at a strike-bound facility from asking delivery drivers, vendors, and outside contractors to honor their picket line.[61] A striking union may ask a union representing employees of a supplier or shipper to instruct its members not to cross.[62]

Exceptions. The law recognizes three situations where the union can picket at a secondary without violating Section 8(b)(4).

• The union can picket struck products being sold by retailers. (See Chapter 4.)

• The union can picket strikebreakers while they work on the premises of a secondary. (See Chapter 7.)

• The union can picket secondaries and induce their employees to stop working if the primary employer refuses to recognize the union or bargain after NLRB certification.[63]

Contractors' gate

In limited circumstances, a struck employer can reserve an entrance at its facility for contractors working on its property. If the gate is properly restricted, the union may not picket.

Prerequisites. A contractors' gate may only be used by contractors who meet both of the following requirements:

1. The contractor must be doing work that is unrelated to the employer's regular operations. An example is the construction of a new building. Contractors overhauling equipment or renovating existing structures are doing related work and do not qualify for insulation.[64] Nor do firms performing security or maintenance functions.

2. The contractor must not be doing work that, if carried out when the plant was operating regularly, would have required a partial or total curtailment of operations. The purpose of this rule is to prevent an employer from taking advantage of a strike.

Polluted gate. If a related-work contractor or a contractor whose activities would ordinarily close the facility uses the reserved gate, the gate is polluted. The gate is also polluted if it is used by employees, suppliers, or customers of the struck employer. The union may picket a polluted gate and appeal for support from all persons going through.[65]

> **Pointer:** To investigate whether a contractor is entitled to a reserved gate, ask the employer for job orders, blueprints, and other relevant documents. If these prove inconclusive, request access to the facility to observe the work.[66]

Common situs picketing

When a struck employer and other employers share a work site, the premises are called a "common situs." Examples: construction sites with multiple contractors; industrial facilities leased to several tenants.

Picketing rules. A union whose employer shares a site with others can picket the site if the struck employer performs or performed bargaining unit work there. The union must, however, take the following steps to reduce the impact on secondaries:

- It must picket as closely as possible to the struck employer's operations.
- Picket signs must clearly identify the struck employer.
- Pickets must not try to affect deliveries to secondary employers or to induce work stoppages by secondary employees.[67]

If the struck employer suspends operations at a common situs, the union can continue to picket if the struck employer stores equipment there or will resume operations when the strike is over.[68]

Dual-gate system. An owner or manager of a common situs can create a dual or reserved-gate system in which one entrance is reserved for the struck employer and another for secondaries. The reserved entrance, called the "primary gate" must be posted with a sign such as the following, restricting its use to the struck employer.

STOP AND READ!
Entrance No. 2 Primary Gate

This entrance is reserved exclusively for the employees, subcontractors, visitors, agents, and suppliers of Heller Cleaning Company. Such persons must use this entrance and no other. All other persons must use Entrance No. 1.

The owner will usually post a second entrance with a sign designating the entrance as a neutral gate and prohibiting its use by the struck employer. The union may not picket the neutral entrance — even if the primary gate is placed in a location far from public view.[69]

> **Pointer:** The union can assign a striker or staff member to monitor the neutral gate to determine if employees or suppliers of the struck employer are using it. The observer cannot walk around or converse with persons going through the entrance but can wear an apron with the legend: "Neutral Gate Observer."

Polluted gate. Employees, customers, suppliers, or subcontractors of the struck employer who use a neutral gate violate the gate system. If the violations form a pattern (generally at least three instances), the union can picket there — until the employer rehabilitates the system by posting new signs, issuing instructions, or posting guards to check identities.[70]

> **Note:** A secondary employee who uses an entrance reserved for a struck employer does not pollute the gate system. Nor is the system compromised if a vendor or a contractor that provides services for the entire site, such as food or sanitation, uses a neutral gate.

Tenants. A struck employer that leases out space may reserve a neutral entrance for its tenants. The union may not picket the tenant entrance unless a tenant using it does related-work business with the struck employer such as buying products, selling materials, or providing services. The union can also picket if employees or agents of the struck employer use the gate.

Employer ULPs

Employer interference with lawful strike activity is an unfair labor practice (ULP). Infractions can change the nature of a stoppage from an economic to a ULP strike. (See Chapter 13.) Where possible, unions should record violations with video cameras.

Violations. It is illegal for an owner, manager, supervisor, or security guard to:

• Threaten or harass lawful picketing
• Summon police to the line without a genuine basis to believe that pickets are violating a law

- Assault a picket, including driving dangerously close to the picket line
- Park heavy machinery or other equipment on sidewalks, streets, or public easements used by pickets
- Run water sprinklers or spread manure to deter picketing
- Display a weapon in a threatening manner, such as standing a shotgun on a car seat
- Write down the names of pickets
- Videotape or pretend to videotape orderly picketing, rallies, or marches
- Threaten physical harm to strikers or their families
- Threaten to fire strikers for name-calling or other minor infractions
- Hire or threaten to hire permanent replacements during a ULP strike
- Threaten to report immigrant strikers to the Department of Homeland Security
- Threaten to permanently subcontract unit work or close the plant if the strike continues
- Threaten to fire strikers or to classify jobs as vacated if strikers do not return by a certain date (but a threat to replace economic strikers is lawful)
- Pull up union signs planted on or tied to public property
- Confiscate barrels, benches, or firewood left on public property or on land owned by a third party
- Suggest to strikers that they would be better off if they got rid of the union or replaced the leadership
- Offer higher wages or other benefits to induce a striker to return to work

    Pointer: When filing ULP charges during a strike, remind the Board agent that the ULP Casehandling Manual requires the Region to investigate whether the ULP caused or is prolonging the walkout.[71]

Court order

It is common practice for employers to record and document picket line incidents. One purpose is to obtain proof for a court injunction. To pad its case, the employer may instruct security guards to provoke strikers.

A court injunction can limit the number of pickets, require them to walk several feet apart, or even forbid patrolling near entrances. Because a judge can jail violators for contempt and impose fines, a court order can break a strike.

Requirements. The evidence needed for a labor injunction depends on the court system where the employer files its request. In the federal courts, the Norris-LaGuardia Anti-Injunction Act requires proof that the union is responsible for unlawful acts that are likely to continue; that the local police are unable or unwilling to provide adequate protection; that the employer is complying with all of its legal obligations, and that the employer is trying to resolve the dispute by negotiations, government mediation, or arbitration.[72]

State courts. Employers usually file injunction requests in state courts, where lower standards may apply. Although 20 states and territories have enacted laws modeled after Norris-LaGuardia,[73] the majority allow judges to issue injunctions on flimsier grounds.

Avoiding an injunction. A union can take several measures to reduce the likelihood of a strike injunction:

- Meet with police before the strike, explain that the union's goals are peaceful, and provide the names and telephone numbers of union officials and the union attorney
- Provide written instructions to pickets
- Conduct training sessions
- Give picket captains the power to remove strikers who block entrances, commit violent acts, carry weapons, or use alcohol
- Provide cameras to picket captains to record employer provocations
- Keep records of misconduct by line crossers, security guards, and supervisors
- Issue press releases and internet postings condemning violent incidents

National emergency injunction. If a strike or a lockout threatens to cause a national emergency, such as the shutdown of a regional port system, the President of the United States can ask a judge to enjoin it for up to 80 days.[74] During the stay, a Board of Inquiry briefs the President on the dispute and the NLRB conducts a vote on the employer's final offer.

Corporate campaign

A strategy that has caught interest in recent years is the corporate campaign. A corporate campaign is a no-holds-barred attack on the employer, its parent entity, and its sister branches and divisions. Since it threatens the employer's very survival, a corporate campaign should not be called in every strike. But it is an appropriate response to an employer who is trying to destroy the union. Tactics include:

- Letters and e-mails to creditors, Wall Street analysts, and the Securities and Exchange Commission conveying unfavorable information about the employer
- Consumer boycotts
- Class-action discrimination and overtime pay lawsuits
- Pollution and hazardous waste complaints
- Requests to legislators to hold hearings on corporate misconduct
- Testimony against property tax exemptions and abatements
- Opposition to building permits and licenses
- Airing grievances at stockholders' meetings
- Exposing the personal and business affairs of directors and major stockholders
- Campaigns against businesses owned by stockholders, directors, and customers
- Encouraging whistle blowers to file triple-damage lawsuits under the Federal False Claims Act

STATE LAW

Q. A state law says unions must give 15 days notice before striking. Are we bound by it?

A. Not if your employer is under the jurisdiction of the National Labor Relations Act. The NLRA pre-empts more restrictive state labor laws.[75]

ROLLING STRIKE

Q. Do we have to call out the entire bargaining unit the first day of the strike?

A. No. You can call a rolling strike, in which one group of workers is called out at a time.[76]

DELIVERY ENTRANCE

Q. Security has marked an entrance with a large sign that says "Neutral Gate – Reserved for Deliveries." Can we picket?

A. Yes. An employer may not create a reserved gate for deliveries to its regular operation.

UNION RESPONSIBILITY

Q. Can the company file ULP charges against the union if pickets threaten scabs?

A. Yes. The NLRA forbids a union from coercing employees.

CALLS TO POLICE

Q. On the first day of the strike, the owner called the police because of illegally parked cars. On the second day he called again to charge that we were following employees home. Later he called a third time and said we were using an illegal scanner. The police came each time but took no action. Can he keep doing this?

A. This depends. An employer can call the police if he has a reasonable concern that strikers are violating a law—even if the police decide that action is not warranted.[77] But he cannot make a deliberately false charge.

MASS PICKETING

Q. If all 85 workers in our bargaining unit picket simultaneously, can the NLRB prosecute the union for mass picketing?

A. This depends. Large-scale picketing is not unlawful in itself. As explained by a federal judge: "Mass picketing stands on the same footing with other picketing as long as it does not block access to and from the struck premises or does not threaten physical violence."[78]

MOVE ON ORDER

Q. We understand the need to keep the picket line moving in the mornings and afternoons when cars are approaching, but how can the police make us keep moving late at night when no one is coming in or out?

A. Laws in some cities and towns require pickets to stay in continuous motion. Otherwise, the police may be exceeding their authority if they force you to patrol when no one is entering or leaving. Discuss the matter with your attorney.

SCAB LAWSUIT

Q. A scab was hit by a rock while leaving the plant. Could he sue the union?

A. This depends. In some states, a scab can sue the union for any picket line assault. But in others, the scab must prove that the union leadership directed or encouraged the attack.

EMPLOYER VIDEOTAPING

Q. On the first day of the strike, picketing was totally peaceful. Yet, we could see a supervisor videotaping us the entire time. Can we file a ULP charge?

A. Yes. Employer agents may not photograph, make sound recordings, or take notes while visibly observing peaceful labor activity. Even the carrying of a camera in public view has been ruled illegal.[79] Video surveillance is permitted only if pickets have engaged in violence, blocking, trespass, dangerous disruptions to traffic, or other serious misconduct.

UNION VIDEOTAPING

Q. Can the union videotape replacement workers?
A. Not necessarily. Since videotaping is coercive, the union must have a legitimate reason, such as a need to document assaults or dangerous driving.

DELAYED ACCEPTANCE

Q. Workers are beginning to desert the strike. To cut our losses, could we simply accept the employer's final contract proposal—which we turned down two weeks ago?
A. Possibly. Unless an employer expressly withdraws an offer after the union's rejection, the union may, within a reasonable time, change its mind and accept.[80]

SUPERVISOR PROFANITY

Q. A supervisor called a striker a "fucking cocksucker." Is this a labor law violation?

A. This depends. Isolated profanity is not unlawful but a practice of repeatedly harassing strikers with obscene comments, curses, or racial slurs, absent equivalent provocation, crosses the line.[81]

JUNK MAIL

Q. The company mailed letters to strikers attacking the union's bargaining demands as "thoughtless and irresponsible." Isn't this a ULP?

A. No, if this is as far as it goes. An employer may mail out its position on negotiations and criticize the union. It may even explain how workers can resign from the union in order to scab on the strike. It commits a ULP, however, if it denigrates union leaders, urges workers to abandon the union, or attempts to pit one part of the bargaining unit against another.[82]

SOLICITING STRIKERS

Q. Can a supervisor call a striker at home and ask her to return?

A. Yes, but the boss may not promise extra benefits such as a jump in pay, a promotion, or superseniority.[83]

ASSAULT BY UNION OFFICIAL

Q. A union officer broke a scab's nose. Could this affect his ability to hold office?

A. Yes. The Landrum-Griffin Act bars a person convicted of serious crimes from serving as a union officer for 13 years. Among the specified offenses is "assault which inflicts grievous bodily injury."[84]

SHUTDOWN

Q. In the third week of the strike, the company notified the union that it was closing the plant for good. Can we sue for back pay under the federal WARN law?

A. No. The federal WARN law, which ordinarily requires 60 days notice prior to a plant shutdown, does not apply to strike-related closings.[85]

WORKERS' COMPENSATION

Q. A striker fell while picketing and injured his leg. Can he collect workers' compensation?

A. No. Injuries incurred by strikers do not come under workers' compensation.

REPLACEMENT LETTER

Q. The employer sent the following letter to 14 strikers: "Because we have hired a permanent replacement for your position, you are no longer employed at A.G. Computers." Can we file ULP charges?

A. Yes. Telling strikers that they are not employed conveys the illegal message that they no longer have reinstatement rights.[86]

SUPERVISORS WORKING OVERTIME

Q. Many supervisors are working 70 hours per week during the strike. They tell us they are only receiving their regular salaries. If this is true, isn't the company violating the overtime law?

A. Yes. If supervisors or managers spend most of their time on production work, the employer must pay them overtime for each hour that exceeds 40.

UI REFERRALS

Q. The state UI office is referring unemployed persons to our employer. Can we do anything about it?

A. Complain to the UI Director. Federal regulations prohibit UI agencies from referring unemployed persons to vacancies created by a strike or a lockout.[87]

BANKRUPTCY

Q. If our employer files for bankruptcy, will we have to stop our strike?

A. No. A union can strike a company that is in bankruptcy.[88]

GENERAL STRIKE

Q. Can other unions in our area support us by calling a general strike like they did in the 1930's?

A. Not safely. For one thing, since World War II, most unions have agreed to contractual no-strike clauses. For another, the Taft-Hartley Act bans a union from picketing or striking to coerce an employer to intervene in another employer's labor dispute.

Chapter 4

Buyer Power

Consumer picketing • Access

Picketing at stores that sell struck products publicizes a strike. It can also take a bite out of the struck employer's profits. The U.S. Supreme Court legalized consumer picketing in a decision known as *Tree Fruits*, explaining that a union does not violate the Taft-Hartley ban on coercive secondary activity if it pickets to ask the public to boycott a struck product, but not the store itself.[89]

Consumer picketing

Unions must follow several rules when conducting consumer picketing:

Signs. Picket signs must clearly identify the targeted product and the struck employer. A sign reading, "Budweiser workers on strike — Boycott Bud" conveys the necessary information. "Don't buy scab beer" does not. On the bottom add: "This is not a strike or boycott against this store."

Store employees. Inducing secondary employees to stop working is illegal, so the union must confine its picketing to customer entrances and to hours when the seller is open for business. Pickets should avoid conversations with store employees and delivery drivers.

CONSUMER PICKETING INSTRUCTIONS

Dear Picket:

We are publicizing a consumer boycott against company products. To make this program a success, please read these instructions and follow them carefully.

1. Picket in a peaceful manner. Do not engage in altercations, arguments, or misconduct of any kind.

2. Picket customer entrances only. If the store is at the rear of a parking lot, or inside a mall, picket on the area immediately in front of the store. If the owner or mall manager tells you to leave, picket at the entrance to the mall or parking lot. In these cases, the union may file charges at the NLRB.

3. Do not picket employee entrances or entrances set aside for deliveries. Avoid conversations with store employees and delivery drivers.

4. As we have no dispute with the store itself, do not make any statements that the store is unfair or on strike. Do not ask customers to boycott the store. We are only asking that they not buy company products.

5. Do not interfere with the work of any employees in the store or any drivers making pickups or deliveries. If anyone asks you what the picketing is about, refer him or her to the picket captain or the union office.

6. Distribute handbills courteously. If customers throw them on the ground, pick them up and keep the area clean.

7. Do not use intoxicating beverages while on duty or have such beverages on your person.

8. If any person complains about your picketing, tell them that you have your instructions and that they should register complaints with the union.

Predominant product. A union may not engage in consumer picketing that could cause a seller ruin or substantial losses.[90] This means the union cannot picket an item which accounts for the predominant portion of a retailer's sales. For example, strikers at a Cadillac manufacturing plant cannot picket an independently owned Cadillac dealership. Nor can the union picket an item that is so merged with other products — for example, paper bags at a grocery store—that a successful customer response would close down the retailer.

> **Note:** At stores where it cannot picket because of the predominant or merged product rules, the union can distribute handbills. Since the union is not picketing, it can urge the public to boycott the entire store. (See Chapter 8.)

Penalties. If a union violates the consumer picketing rules, the employer or the seller can file ULP charges or sue the union in court.

Access

A frequent problem in consumer picketing is getting close enough to entrances so that customers can see the picket signs and the union can distribute leaflets. The problem is worst when the store is inside a shopping mall.

Lechmere. Union rights to conduct consumer picketing and handbilling on private property were limited by the Supreme Court's *Lechmere* decision.[91] *Lechmere* stands for the rule that a store or mall owner may refuse access to a union unless it regularly allows other outside organizations to solicit on its premises.

If a store or mall owner orders the union to move from outside the store, and the union has evidence that other groups have been permitted to set up tables or hand out literature, the union should file a ULP charge.[92]

PEPSI'S THE ONE

Q. Our company makes the aluminum that Pepsi-Cola uses in its soft drink cans. Can we picket grocery stores to ask customers not to buy Pepsi?

A. Yes, if you confine your appeal to Pepsi in cans.

COMMUNICATIONS WITH STORE MANAGERS

Q. We are striking a company that manufactures potato chips and pretzels. Can we ask store managers not to carry these items and warn them that otherwise we will picket?

A. Yes. But you must make clear that you will restrict your picketing to struck products. A broad threat to "picket the store" is illegal.

STATE LAW

Q. A law in our state forbids picketing at workplaces where no strike is in progress. Does this prevent us from picketing struck products?

A. No. The doctrine of federal preemption overrides state laws that interfere with conduct protected by the National Labor Relations Act.

TAKE DOWN CONDITION

Q. Can we tell a storeowner that if he stops selling a struck product, we will take down our picket line?

A. Yes.

WHOLESALER

Q. Our company sells pool tables to wholesalers who sell them to retailers. Can we picket the wholesalers?

A. Probably not. The consumer picketing doctrine was developed to respond to retail store picketing. It has not been applied to wholesalers or distributors.

Chapter 5

Extending the Strike

Common enterprises • Struck work • Foreign connections

A llies of a struck employer are not included in the Taft-Hartley ban on secondary picketing. A union can picket an ally with "On strike" signs, ask employees not to work, and turn away deliveries.

A common-sense listing of allies would include customers, suppliers, contractors, investors, financing institutions, and entities owned in common. Not surprisingly, the NLRB takes a more narrow approach. It limits the ally designation to (1) entities that are so integrated with the struck employer that they form a common enterprise; and (2) entities that perform struck work.

Common enterprises

The issue of common enterprise status arises when a union considers picketing another branch or division of the same corporation. It also arises when the union considers picketing businesses owned by the owner or the owner's family. There is no bright-line test to determine whether two entities form a common enterprise. Instead, the NLRB asks the following questions:

- Are the entities under common ownership or financial control?
- Are the labor relations policies of the entities commonly or centrally controlled?
- Are the entities' operations interrelated?
- Are the entities under common management?

Applying the factors. Common ownership or financial control is a requirement for a common enterprise. Also crucial are common labor relations policies and interrelatedness. Common management is the least important factor.

If a parent entity closely supervises the labor policies of its subsidiaries, and if the subsidiaries do business with each other or interchange personnel, the subsidiaries and the parent can be classified as a common enterprise — even if each is separately incorporated and managed.

> **Example:** Huttig Door Co. owned two separately incorporated branches in Montana and South Carolina. A Huttig vice president supervised labor relations activities at the branches and attended negotiating sessions. The Montana branch supplied 50 to 60 per cent of the South Carolina branch's components and they exchanged equipment between them. Based on these facts, and other evidence of interrelatedness, the NLRB ruled that the two branches were allies. This allowed workers on strike in South Carolina to picket in Montana.[93]

On the other hand, when a parent entity allows its subsidiaries to function autonomously, with local responsibility for labor relations policies, the subsidiaries and the parent are not common enterprises.

> **Example:** The Hearst Corporation owned newspapers in Los Angeles and San Francisco. Neither paper was incorporated but each had authority to decide its own wages and work rules. Headquarters gave advice on collective bargaining but did not participate in negotiations or approve final contracts. Due to the absence of centralized labor policies, the Board ruled that the papers were not allies. Strikers in Los Angeles could not picket in San Francisco.[94]

Considerations. Because the Board's ally methodology is imprecise, a union takes a chance when it pickets other businesses. The best policy is to gather as much information as possible (hopefully well in advance of contract expiration) and discuss the matter with counsel.

Even when common enterprise status is nose-on-your-face plain, the union must consider the workers at the sister facility. If their collective bargaining agreement bars sympathy strikes, honoring an outside union's picket line could subject employees to discharges and their union to a lawsuit. In a 1990 case, Iowa workers picketed a branch of their corporation in South Dakota. When the South Dakota workers honored the picket line, the South Dakota company sued the South Dakota union and won a judgment of $24.6 million.[95]

Struck work

The second group of allies are persons and employers that perform struck work. Struck work is work which, but for the strike, would have been handled by strikers. A union can picket a company doing struck work and attempt to close it down.

Who initiates? To create a struck work relationship, the struck employer must arrange for an outside business to take over its duties. If a customer initiates the move, the outside business is not an ally.[96]

> **Example:** Smelly Bakery makes the dough for Mama's Pizza. When the workers at Smelly went on strike, Mama's contracted with Tasty Bakery to supply pizza dough. Can the Smelly strikers picket Tasty? No, because the customer, not Smelly, made the arrangements.

Information request. A striking union may be in the dark about whether its employer is farming out and, if so, to whom. One tactic is to submit an information request asking for the names of outside companies doing bargaining unit work.[97]

Foreign connections

If the struck employer has a foreign branch, or if it sells to foreign customers, members may suggest sending a delegation to picket. But the Taft-Hartley Act bans secondary picketing by U.S. unions anywhere on the globe and if a foreign operation manages its labor policies without close supervision from the United States, it may not be a common enterprise.

International solidarity. Instead of sending workers, could the union ask a foreign union to picket in its place? In a 1993 case, the Board said no, contending that when a foreign union responds to a request by a U.S. union, it becomes an agent of the U.S. union.[98] The Court of Appeals for the District of Columbia rejected this thesis, stating:

> We discern nothing in the law of agency to support a theory transforming one union into the agent of another based upon the spirit of labor solidarity standing alone.[99]

Despite the D.C. Circuit, the Board has not announced a retreat from its dubious agency theory. Unless it does, solidarity requests should be made orally and the U.S. union should not help in picket planning or execution.

LOCATIONS

Q. Our employer is farming out work to a firm that has three facilities. Can we picket each?

A. Not necessarily. The Board appears to restrict picketing to locations where struck work is performed.[100]

TEMP AGENCY

Q. Our company has contracted with Labor Ready for strike replacements. Can we picket the agency?

A. This depends. If Labor Ready is simply referring applicants, it is not an ally under the law. But if the replacements remain on the agency's payroll, the agency is doing your work.

TAXI COMPANY

Q. Can we picket the headquarters of a taxi company that is driving scabs into the plant?

A. No. A secondary does not become an ally by assisting an employer with temporary strike measures (unless it is performing strikers' work).

SINGLE CUSTOMER

Q. Our company only has one customer: General Electric Company. Is GE an ally?

A. No.

TENANTS

Q. We are striking a contractor who cleans downtown offices. Many tenants are doing their own vacuuming during the strike. Does this open them up for picketing?

A. No. A customer that voluntarily assumes tasks formerly done by strikers is not an ally.[101]

STORAGE FACILITY

Q. Our company stores products in a public warehouse. Can we picket?

A. Not unless warehouse workers are performing duties formerly performed by strikers.

PERSONAL LIABILITY

Q. If we make a mistake and picket a secondary, could the secondary sue the union's officers for money damages?

A. No. Individual officers or members cannot be held personally liable for secondary picketing violations.[102]

Chapter 6

Making It Personal

Residential picketing • Strikebreakers

Picketing the homes of owners, officers, and directors adds a unique dimension to a strike. It embarrasses bosses in front of their neighbors and visitors and provides a good way for strikers' family members to assist the struggle.

Residential picketing

Conducted in a peaceful and orderly fashion, picketing the residences of owners, officers, trustees, directors, and stockholders is protected Section 7 activity.[103] The union must, however, pay heed to local picketing laws.

Local picketing laws. In a 1988 decision known as Frisby, the Supreme Court said that local governments can forbid picketing "taking place solely in front of a particular residence."[104] Many localities have since enacted "targeted" picketing restrictions, mainly to shield doctors from aggressive anti-abortion protesters. These laws generally forbid picketing unless the participants walk past several houses at a time. For example, a Colorado ordinance provides that:

> It shall be unlawful for any person to engage in targeted picketing in a residential area, except when such person is engaging in targeted picketing while marching, without stopping in front of a residence, over a route that proceeds along the entire one-way length of at least one block of a street.[105]

Some cities ban picketing within a specified number of feet from the target's home. If the distance is 50 feet or so, the ordinance is probably valid. Greater distances may be unconstitutional.[106]

Statutes in Arizona, Arkansas, Hawaii, Illinois, and Virginia prohibit "picketing before or about the residence or dwelling place of any individual." Michigan, Minnesota, and Nebraska have similar laws. Under *Frisby* it would appear that these must be narrowly construed, for example, to bar picketing in front of a single residence but to allow it if the line passes a group of homes.[107] Unions in these states should consult with counsel.

Conduct. Residential pickets should not engage in vulgar language, loud behavior, or threats. Conversations with neighborhood children should be avoided.

Signs. Picket signs can condemn the employer's policies and labor law violations. Handbills can list the owner's name and telephone number and urge neighbors to call.

Lawsuit. If the union pickets repeatedly, the homeowner may petition for a court injunction based on invasion of privacy. Local judges often cooperate. Here is how one justified shutting down a picket line:

> Truly it is shocking, reprehensible and outrageous, deserving the unhesitating and scathing rebuke of the court. Conducted at a considerable distance from the hospital, in an exclusively residential area, it was apparently aimed to cause unspeakable embarrassment, humiliation, and mortification … it represents a form of direct and unmitigated coercion and terrorism … a mean, foul and sinister blow … jungle tactics and indiscriminate warfare.[108]

Strikebreakers

Section 8(b)(1)(A) of the NLRA prohibits a union from using coercive tactics against strikebreakers.[109] Picketing residences has been ruled a violation where picket signs labeled the worker as a scab, large numbers took part, and pickets antagonized family members.[110] Section 8(b)(1)(A) does not apply to owners or directors.

WEDDING FESTIVITIES

Q. The owner's daughter is getting married in a fancy hotel. Can we set up a picket line?

A. Not safely. Since the hotel is a secondary employer, picketing risks Section 8(b)(4) charges.[111] Handbilling is a better bet.

DIRECTOR

Q. Our company's Board of Directors includes many prominent business-people. Can we picket their homes and places of work?

A. Picketing homes is lawful, but not places of work.

BANK PRESIDENT

Q. A local bank lends to our company. Can we picket the bank president's home?

A. No. The bank and its president are secondaries.[112]

Chapter 7

Follow that Truck!

Moore Dry Dock rules • Additional precautions

I n ambulatory picketing the union follows or tracks supervisors, non-strikers, and replacements and pickets them while they work offsite, even if this is at a secondary business or residence. Conducted properly, ambulatory (known also as mobile or roving) picketing is a lawful means to try to shut down a struck employer.

Moore Dry Dock rules

A union that pickets scabs while they work on the premises of a secondary must follow four rules called the Moore Dry Dock standards. Divergence is regarded as evidence that the union's purpose is to coerce the secondary to stop doing business with the struck employer. This opens the union to a ULP charge and a lawsuit. The rules are:

1. The union must only picket when a person doing bargaining unit work is on the secondary's premises.

2. The scab must be engaged in the struck employer's normal business.

3. The union must picket as close as possible to where the scab is working.

4. Picket signs must clearly identify the struck employer.

Presence. Under the first *Dry Dock* rule, the union must wait to picket until a scab enters the secondary's premises and must disperse when he or she leaves for the day, even if the scab leaves vehicles or equipment on site.

> **Pointer:** Some secondaries send scabs out a back exit and then videotape the union's "illegal" picket line. To foil this scheme, assign observers to watch the exits. One union rented a small plane and flew over a site to confirm that scabs were still on the premises!

Normal operations. The scab must be performing duties that are consistent with the struck employer's normal business. The union cannot picket a restaurant because a scab is eating there.

Proximity. To satisfy the third *Dry Dock* rule, the union must ask the secondary for permission to enter the premises and picket near where the scab is working. Only if the secondary ignores or refuses the request can the union picket the outside entrance nearest the work.[113] If the secondary creates a reserved gate for the strikebreakers, the union must picket at this location.

> **Pointer:** Send certified letters to customers requesting permission to picket inside when scabs arrive. (See sample on page 72.) No response counts as disapproval, allowing you to picket outside without asking again.[114]

Signs. Ambulatory picket signs must name the struck employer, not the secondary. On the bottom, write: "This picketing is not intended to induce any other person to cease work." Placards that simply say "On strike" or "Unfair" are inadequate.

Additional precautions

A union that obeys the *Dry Dock* standards is not home free. It must avoid any other conduct that suggests that it is trying to pressure the secondary.

To this end, pickets should not:

- Ask employees of the secondary employer, or unions representing secondary employees, to stop work
- Record the names or license plate numbers of secondary employees who cross the picket line
- Call secondary employees scabs
- Restrict picketing to unionized locations
- Take pictures of scab vehicles as they enter or leave the facility
- Ask customers or persons making deliveries to the secondary employer to respect the picket line
- Take breaks when no cars or trucks are approaching

Silence is not golden. If a secondary employee asks the reason for the picketing, and the picket fails to answer, the NLRB may take this as evidence that the union's purpose is to induce the employee to honor the picket line. Instruct pickets to say, "This will explain," and to offer a union leaflet.

INSTRUCTIONS
for Ambulatory Pickets

The National Labor Relations Act (NLRA) permits us to picket Dawson Trucking, not only at its principal place of business but wherever employees are doing bargaining unit work. Because many supervisors and replacements spend time away from Dawson's premises, we must picket at customer terminals and loading docks. This is called ambulatory picketing. To avoid subjecting the union to secondary boycott charges, it is very important that you follow these instructions:

1. The union will give you a letter directed to the customer upon whose premises Dawson makes deliveries or picks up goods. This letter will ask the customer to permit you to enter the premises so that you may picket the Dawson truck and driver as closely as possible.

2. Present the letter to someone in authority, if not the general manager or a supervisor, then a guard at the front gate.

3. If the customer gives you permission, enter the premises and picket as close to the truck and driver as possible. Do not picket anywhere else on the property.

4. If you are refused permission, picket the entrance closest to where the scab employee is working. If the terminal establishes a reserved gate for Dawson, picket that gate and call the union.

5. Do not talk with employees of the customer or another secondary. Do not even say "good morning."

6. Do not tell secondary employees that an outside labor body has sanctioned the strike.

7. The union will give you a picket sign that will make clear that your picketing is directed only against Dawson. Do not use any other signs.

8. Do not ask secondary persons seeking to enter the site to honor the line. Do not call them scabs.

9. Unless you are picketing at a reserved gate, do not stop picketing between the arrival of vehicles or persons.

10. The union will give you handbills. If someone asks you about the picketing, respond by saying, "This will explain," and offer them a handbill. Do not wink or give any other signal to stop work.

11. Leave the job site when the Dawson driver completes his business. Do not picket unless you are certain that a Dawson driver (not simply a Dawson truck) is still on the premises.

REQUEST TO ENTER

To whom it may concern:

Teamsters Local 728 is currently on strike against Dawson Trucking. Federal law entitles us to picket Dawson not only at its principal place of business but also wherever its employees are working. We are following drivers who work for Dawson and picketing them while they make pickups and deliveries. We have no dispute with you or any employer other than Dawson.

We request permission to come onto your premises to picket as close as possible to the Dawson driver and truck. We will picket only when a Dawson driver is present.

Please inform us whether we have your permission to enter the premises for the above purposes. If you do not respond, we will assume that permission is denied.

PICKET SIGN

TEAMSTERS LOCAL 728 ON STRIKE AGAINST DAWSON TRUCKING FOR UNFAIR LABOR PRACTICES

This picketing is not directed toward the employees of any other employer.

HANDBILL

Teamsters Local 728 is on strike against Dawson Trucking. Our union has no dispute with companies with which Dawson is interchanging freight or otherwise doing business.

The drivers for Dawson spend most of their time away from the Dawson premises. This makes it necessary for us to picket them where they work. This picketing is directed only at the drivers of Dawson Trucking and is not an appeal for any other workers to stop work.

QUESTIONS & ANSWERS

TRAILING TRUCKS

Q. Can we be fired for trailing scab trucks?

A. No. Trailing strikebreakers to offsite work locations is protected unless you tailgate or engage in other intimidating maneuvers.[115]

SYMPATHY WALKOUT

Q. We picketed a cement truck while it unloaded at a construction site. This led the carpenters to walk off the job. Can we be sued for causing a secondary strike?

A. Not if your picketing conformed to the *Dry Dock* standards and no picket asked or signaled a carpenter to stop work. Ambulatory or common situs picketing is not unlawful merely because neutral employees respect the picket line.[116]

REQUEST TO ENTER

Q. A truck we were following drove into a department store delivery bay. Can we set up a line at the entrance?

A. Yes, but first you must ask for permission to enter the facility to picket "between the headlights."

LUNCH HOUR

Q. When the scabs take breaks, do we have to shut down the line?

A. No. Picketing may continue while targeted employees temporarily stop work for lunch, coffee breaks, or personal needs.[117]

REQUEST NOT TO UNLOAD

Q. While picketing a delivery to a warehouse, can we ask warehouse employees not to unload the scab truck?

A. Yes, but take care. You can ask secondary workers to respect your picket line by not performing services that aid the struck employer, such as unloading.[118] But you may not ask them to leave the premises or to stop work entirely. Nor may you ask them not to handle the merchandise once it is off the truck.

WARNING LETTER

Q. Can we write to a business which contracts with our company and warn that if scabs enter the premises we will send strikers to picket?

A. Yes, but you must make clear that your picketing will conform to the *Dry Dock* standards. For instance, you could warn that "if a scab truck arrives at your facility, we will picket as close as we can to it."

Chapter 8

Taking It to the Secondary

Handbilling • Bannering • "Rodenting" • Demonstrating • Other tactics

For many years after its passage, the Taft-Hartley Act's restrictions on secondary activity appeared to be all encompassing. But in a 1988 decision known as *DeBartolo*, the Supreme Court begrudgingly acknowledged that handbilling and other nonpicketing publicity against secondaries is allowed by the Act.[119] *DeBartolo* gives unions a green light to put pressure on buyers, suppliers, contractors, banks, sister branches, advertisers, sellers, property owners, tenants, government agencies, and other entities that do business with a struck employer or are in a position to influence it.

Handbilling

As long as a striking union refrains from picketing, it can distribute handbills that condemn a secondary, criticize its products or services, and ask
the public to withhold patronage. Advertisements can be purchased to the
same effect. The union can leaflet in front of the secondary's place of business or in areas where the public gathers, such as sports stadiums or trans-
port hubs.

> **Example:** The main customer of a cleaning company struck by Local 399
> was Delta Air Lines. To put pressure on Delta, the union handbilled at
> airline terminals. One side of the leaflet said: "Please do not fly Delta
> Airlines. Delta Airlines unfair, does not provide AFL-CIO conditions of
> employment." The other side criticized Delta's safety record and warned,
> "It takes more than money to fly Delta. It takes nerve." Delta filed charges
> at the NLRB claiming the campaign was illegal secondary activity but the
> Board said the handbills were lawful under *DeBartolo*.[120]

> **Pointer:** Before starting a boycott campaign, visit or send a letter to the
> secondary, warning that the union will handbill unless the customer sus-
> pends its business dealings. If you get no response, send a second letter
> enclosing the handbill. If the secondary has a union, contact it to solicit
> support (short of striking or refusing to handle products).

Conduct. To reach motorists driving into a secondary's parking lot,
handbillers may walk across entrances, flag down cars, and talk with drivers. They can wear brightly colored T-shirts with boycott messages on the
front and back, ring bells, use bullhorns, or even display a giant banner
(see next section). But they may not patrol, argue with customers or delivery persons, hold leaflets above or in front of their bodies like signs,
gather in large groups, or ask anyone to stop working. See sample instructions on page 77.

Content. Although not an absolute requirement, a handbill has a better
chance of surviving a legal attack if it identifies the struck employer and its
connections with the secondary. On the bottom, add: "This appeal is
directed only to the general public. We are not asking any person to cease
work or to stop making deliveries."

INSTRUCTIONS FOR HANDBILLERS

The National Labor Relations Act (NLRA) and the U.S. Constitution guarantee the right of union members to handbill a business that trades with a struck employer, provides it with services, sells its products, or assists it in other ways. The union can ask customers to support its struggle by refusing to buy products or services. The law, however, does not permit picketing or picketing-like activity. Please follow these instructions.

Don'ts

- Don't congregate in groups; no more than one or two handbillers should stand at a door or entrance.
- Don't mill around without handbills.
- Don't walk back and forth or act in any other manner that could be construed as patrolling.
- Don't get into arguments.
- Don't force handbills on anyone.
- Don't wave handbills, hold them over your head, or grip them against your chest like placards.
- Don't block entrances or exits.
- Don't shout, use profanity, threaten violence, or call persons names.
- Don't advise anyone to strike. If a driver asks whether he should make a delivery on the premises, say yes.
- Don't threaten to picket. Don't even use the word picket.
- Don't litter.
- Don't videotape customers or employees.

Do's

- Do explain why you are handbilling: "Employees at Miller Furniture have been forced out on an unfair-labor-practice strike because the Company wants to take away our union rights. This store supports Miller by buying its products. We are asking you to exercise your conscience as a consumer by boycotting the store."
- Do leave the premises immediately if, for any reason, you fear for your safety.

Bannering

Instead of, or along with, handbills, a union can display a large banner or billboard addressed to the public. Possible legends: "Please Don't Shop Here," or "Shame on Delta Airlines."[121]

Truthfulness. The banner should not imply that the secondary is involved in a dispute with its own employees. "On strike for better wages" gives a false impression. A better legend: "Shame on General Motors."

Numbers. Forcing shoppers or secondary employees to run a gauntlet of banners is coercive. A single banner is better. The banner must remain stationary.

Location. Do not place the banner in front of an employee entrance or driveway.

Disclaimer. On the bottom of the banner, print: "This banner is addressed exclusively to the public and is not intended to cause any employees to refuse to perform services or to deliver goods."

"Rodenting"

A popular technique in the building trades is to fly a large rat balloon at the site of a secondary employer and to dress handbillers in rat costumes. At first, the NLRB recognized the activity as lawful. But in recent years the General Counsel has contended that rats are a signal to secondary employees to walk out.

A skunk figure is safer. According to the NLRB Division of Advice: "A skunk, unlike a rat, has no historical significance in the labor movement and does not, by its mere display, operate as a signal to employees or passers-by to take any particular action."[122]

Demonstrating

Holding a demonstration or rally at the premises of a secondary employer is lawful unless the activity disrupts operations, impedes persons from entering, or is otherwise confrontational. The union should:

• Keep demonstrators to 50 or less
• Avoid signs

• Instruct participants to stay in one place
• Demonstrate outside hours when secondary employees enter or exit
• Demonstrate away from entrances

Other tactics

The following activities have been ruled coercive:

• Protesters handcuffing themselves to the doors of a building owned by a secondary
• Dumping trash bags filled with shredded paper in a secondary's lobby
• Blasting a sound system outside a secondary
• "Shop-ins" at stores selling struck products
• Conducting a mock funeral procession in front of a secondary's entrance

On the other hand, if the group does not come to rest before any particular establishment, the union can parade downtown with signs asking the public to boycott a secondary.[123]

SHOPPING MALL

Q. When we tried to distribute boycott flyers in a shopping mall in front of a store selling struck products, the mall manager called the cops to kick us out. Do we have any rights?

A. This depends. A mall or store owner can bar an outside union from handbilling on its property unless it allows other groups or organizations to solicit on a frequent or extended basis.[124]

BOYCOTT THREAT

Q. Can we visit a business that buys from our company, ask the owner to stop making purchases during the strike, and threaten to organize a boycott if he refuses?

A. Yes, if you confine your threats to handbilling or other nonpicketing publicity.[125]

CHARITY BEGINS AT HOME

Q. The president of our company serves on the boards of two charities. Could we buy advertisements asking the public not to donate to these organizations until she agrees to a contract?

A. Yes.

PROXIMITY TO PICKETING

Q. We picketed a business we thought was a subsidiary. They say they are a separate business. Can we change to handbilling?

A. Not right away. The Board usually insists that a union suspend handbilling for a period of time after illegal picketing unless the picketing was brief.[126]

ENVIRONMENTAL COMPLAINT

Q. Can we file an EPA complaint over a secondary's environmental practices?

A. Yes, if you have a reasonable basis for a charge.[127]

PUSHING THE ENVELOPE

Q. Our company's largest customer is a nonunion manufacturer. Leaflets and banners will have little effect because it does not sell to the public. Is there any way for us to picket?

A. The safe answer is no, since picketing a secondary is almost always illegal. If you are willing to take risks, however, consider the following techniques. But take heed: some of these could lead to lawsuits or NLRB charges. Consult with counsel.

- You could handbill and banner on the apron of the manufacturer's driveway (the part which is on the public right-of-way). If the company orders you off or calls the police, you could file a ULP charge alleging unlawful interference with your Section 7 rights; then picket with signs protesting the unfair labor practice.
- You could send members wearing union shirts or jackets to apply for work. If the customer turns them down, you could file discrimination charges at the NLRB and picket the company in protest.
- You could ask a student or community group to picket.
- You could encourage another union to begin a drive at the customer involving recognitional or area standards picketing.

COUNTERATTACK

Q. We handbilled a business owned by a company director. The next day the director's lawyer sent us a letter threatening to sue for "tortious interference with business relations." Do we have to stop?

A. No. Except in narrow circumstances, activity protected by the NLRA, such as truthful labor dispute handbilling, cannot be the subject of a tort lawsuit.[128]

Chapter 9

Honor thy Line

Nonunion supporters • *Union members*

When a worker from outside the bargaining unit respects a picket line, he or she is called a "sympathy striker." A worker who refuses to assume a striker's job duties is also a member of this honorable family.

Nonunion supporters

Office staff, engineers, guards, and other nonunion employees may not know it, but the National Labor Relations Act (NLRA) affords them a protected right to support fellow workers.[129] An employer cannot punish a nonunion worker for honoring a lawful picket line, whether the worker's reason is to show support, to remain neutral, or simply to avoid an unpleasant confrontation.[130]

Replacement. Although an employer may not fire a nonunion employee for respecting a picket line, it can replace the employee to the same extent that it can replace the worker he or she is supporting. If the worker honors a picket line of economic strikers, the employer can hire a permanent replacement. In that event, when the strike concludes, the worker must be placed on a preferential recall list until a suitable vacancy emerges. If the worker honors a picket line of ULP strikers (see Chapter 13), the employer must give the worker his or her job back on request.

This suggests the following exchange:

Sally *(nonunion office worker)*: Tom, I support your people 100 percent and it makes me sick to cross the line, but what protection do I have? You know as well as I do that if I stay out they will replace me in a heartbeat.

Tom *(union president)*: I appreciate what you're saying, Sally, and I want you to do what you feel is right. I cannot guarantee anything, but I can tell you that the union and its attorneys believe we are on an unfair-labor-practice strike. If we're right, you'll be entitled to your job back when the strike is over. We promise to go to bat for you, both at the bargaining table and at the NLRB.

Unemployment insurance. Sympathy strikers normally do not qualify for unemployment insurance, though some states award benefits if an employee refuses to cross a picket line because of a fear of physical harm.[131] Notification of permanent replacement, however, generally triggers UI eligibility.

Supervisors. The NLRA does not protect supervisors. They can be discharged for honoring a picket line.

Union members

If there are two bargaining units in a workplace and one unit hits the bricks, can the other honor the picket line?

A related question: a union driver arrives at a struck workplace to deliver supplies. Can he or she be fired for honoring the picket line?

What does the contract say? As explained above, the NLRA protects employees who honor other workers' picket lines. But there is a catch: If the honoring worker is subject to a union contract that prohibits sympathy strikes, NLRA safeguards do not apply.

Determining whether a labor agreement prohibits sympathy strikes requires an examination of the honoring worker's contract, in particular, its no-strike and picket-line clauses. The three most common patterns are express ban, express authorization, and ambiguous ban.

Express ban. The following no-strike language expressly bans sympathy strike activity:

> The union agrees that there shall be no strike of any kind, including a sympathy strike, slowdown, stoppage of work, sickout, sit-in, or delay of work during the term of this agreement.

By its explicit reference to sympathy strikes, the clause clearly bars employees from honoring picket lines. The employer can fire an employee who refuses to work. If the union encourages violations, the employer can sue for breach of contract.

There are only two exceptions to an express ban on sympathy strikes. The first is where a serious unfair labor practice, such as a refusal to bargain, precipitated the strike being honored. In this circumstance, the NLRA protects sympathy strikers unless language in the contract clearly bans ULP strikes.[132]

The second is Section 502 of the NLRA. This law says that a refusal to to work to avoid "abnormally dangerous" working conditions is not a strike.[133] Crossing a picket line is abnormally dangerous if pickets have threatened or assaulted line crossers.[134]

Express authorization. Some contracts, especially in the transportation industry, grant workers clear permission to honor picket lines. For example, Article 9 of the Teamsters' National Master Freight Agreement reads as follows:

> It shall not be a violation of this agreement and it shall not be cause for discharge, disciplinary action, or permanent replacement in the event an employee refuses to enter upon any property involving a primary labor dispute, or refuses to go through or work behind any primary picket line, including the primary picket line of unions party to this agreement, and including picket lines at the employer's place of business.

Article 9 allows employees to respect picket lines at home and on assignment. It also prohibits an employer from permanently replacing a sympathy

striker. Teamster contracts with UPS contain similar language.

The Master Freight and UPS agreements are a boon for unions that want Teamster drivers to respect their picket lines. But it is a mistake to assume too much. Some local Teamsters' contracts do not have a picket line clause. Some drivers are unaware of their contractual rights. Finally, it is not uncommon for a driver to park near a struck facility, call dispatch to register an objection, and be instructed to wait while a supervisor or a scab takes the truck through the picket line.

Ambiguous ban. The following clause is ambiguous about sympathy strikes:

> There shall be no strikes, stoppages, slowdowns, picketing, or lockouts during the term of this agreement.

Because this language does not explicitly refer to sympathy strikes, it is open to two opposing interpretations: that the parties intended "no strikes" to include sympathy strikes; or that the failure to mention sympathy strikes reveals the parties' intent to permit such activity.

A past arbitration or NLRB decision may have interpreted the clause. If not, and employees are disciplined for honoring a picket line, the following facts will support a union claim that the contract permits sympathy strikes:

- Prior incidents of workers respecting picket lines without employer discipline
- Failed attempts by the employer to bargain an express ban on sympathy strikes
- The location of the no-strike clause within the grievance-arbitration article
- The negotiation of the clause between 1978 and 1985 (when the Board tended to rule that ambiguous no-strike clauses did not bar sympathy strikes)

The following facts will support an employer contention that sympathy strikes are forbidden:

- Past incidents of discipline for respecting a picket line
- A failed attempt by the union to secure an express authorization for workers to honor picket lines
- Instructions by the union to call off a sympathy strike and return to work
- The placement of the no-strike clause in an article separate from the grievance-arbitration procedure
- The negotiation of the clause before 1978 or after 1985

STRUCK WORK

Q. The day we struck, the company asked the nonunion office staff to work production. Can they fire a bookkeeper for refusing?

A. Not legally. A nonunion employee has a protected right to reject struck work if she is willing to perform her regular duties.[135]

LAWSUIT AGAINST UNION

Q. The company is suing the union for $2 million for illegally honoring another union's picket line. If the company wins, could it attach the union's future dues collections?

A. Theoretically, yes, although the union may be able to escape the dilemma by filing for bankruptcy protection.[136]

CONTRACT EXPIRATION

Q. Our bargaining agreement, which prohibits sympathy strikes, expired last month and we are working without a contract. If another union in our facility goes on strike, could we honor its line?

A. Yes. When a contract expires, so does the no-strike clause.

HOSPITAL

Q. If the hospital technicians strike, would the nurse's union have to give ten days notice before honoring the picket line?

A. Yes. Section 8(g) of the NLRA, which applies at health care institutions, bars a union from picketing or striking without ten days advance notice.

OUTSIDE UNIONS

Q. A hospital union put out a call for outside unions to join them on the picket line. Do the other unions have to file ten-day notices with the hospital and the FMCS?

A. Yes. Section 8(g) applies to any union that pickets against a health care institution.

Chapter 10

Benefit Daze

Health insurance • Unemployment benefits • Vacation pay • Disability pay

Cutting off health insurance is an assault against strikers. Applying for unemployment benefits can be a blow against the employer. Benefit issues often affect the course of a strike.

Health insurance

The NLRB views health insurance as a reward for current service, not as an accrued benefit. Consequently, when a strike begins, or at any point thereafter, an employer can unilaterally cease making premium contributions or providing benefits as a self-insurer.[137]

Some union-administered health and welfare funds cover strikers for a few weeks or months. Some unions earmark special funds to help members who incur large medical expenses. And some members can secure coverage under a spouse's plan. But for many, the bleak choices are: pay for COBRA continuation coverage, try to qualify for Medicaid, or take a chance and go without.

COBRA. A federal law known as "COBRA" permits a striker to stay in a group health plan for up to 18 months.[138] But the striker must pay the entire monthly premium, plus up to two percent for administrative expenses. To reduce the burden, the worker can change from family to single coverage, drop dependents, cover dependents only, cover a specific dependent only, or forego dental and vision benefits.

Procedures. Health plan administrators must promptly inform strikers and their beneficiaries when the employer stops payments. The notice must explain the employee's right to become a self-payer.

Employees must be allowed 60 calendar days to elect self-paying status from the last day of employer benefits or the date of the COBRA notice, whichever is later, and a 45-day grace period to mail the first premium. Thus, the earliest an employee can be compelled to mail a check is 105 days after a strike begins.

> **Example:** Judy Fox's union went on strike on June 1. On June 15, the health plan administrator notified her that her employer stopped its coverage on the first day of the strike and she must make a COBRA election within 60 days. If Fox waits until the last day to elect, August 15, she will have 45 days, until September 30, to mail her first premium.

Notice to providers. During COBRA election and grace periods, health plan administrators must respond to inquiries from providers by explaining that a striker has conditional health plan coverage, dependent solely on the worker submitting a premium payment within the allowable time. An administrator who advises a provider that a striker or beneficiary is not covered is subject to a cash penalty.[139]

> **Pointer:** The high cost of health insurance—often more than $1,000 a month for a family—makes COBRA unthinkable for many workers. One option is to wait close to 105 days to see if the strike settles. If it doesn't, and your family has not incurred significant medical expenses, consider going without until the strike settles. Another option is joining a new plan. But take heed: a gap of 63 days without coverage will allow a new plan to exclude pre-existing conditions for a period. You may want to buy enough coverage to make the transition with less than a 63-day gap.

Medicaid. Strikers may be able to qualify for state Medicaid benefits if they have a child or pregnant person in their household. Income and asset requirements vary. Some states are relatively generous, covering households without regard to assets. Others, particularly in the South, impose strict income and asset tests or disqualify two-adult households. Approved families normally receive coverage going back three months before the filing date. The union should research state requirements prior to striking.

Unemployment benefits

Each state administers an unemployment insurance (UI) program. Most disqualify strikers, but there are exceptions.

New York. New York turns down strikers for seven weeks. The eighth week counts as the waiting period. Benefits are paid in the ninth.

West Virginia. West Virginia awards UI benefits if a strike protests wages, hours, or conditions that are "substantially less favorable" than those of similar workers in the same locality.

Stoppage states. In 18 states and Puerto Rico (see box on next page), UI programs only disqualify if the strike is causing a "stoppage of work." If operations continue, strikers can collect.

Most UI programs define a stoppage of work as a substantial curtailment of operations, normally at least 20 to 30 percent, compared with the same week or month the previous year. This allows strikers to qualify if the employer maintains operations at the 70 to 80 percent mark or restores production to this level.

> **Example:** A Massachusetts company continued work during a strike with supervisors, retired managers, and white-collar workers. In the first month, output was 20 percent of the previous year. In the second month, output was 42 percent. In the third, production rose to 75 percent, qualifying strikers for UI benefits.[140]

Employers sometimes argue that even though they are maintaining full output, they are experiencing a stoppage because personnel transfers to fill in for the strikers are impacting maintenance, inspection, research, or other support functions. Proof of substantial disruption is required. One court ruled: "[A] stoppage of work requires more than the holes in cover-

---

WORK-STOPPAGE STATES AND TERRITORIES

Alaska, Delaware, Georgia, Hawaii, Illinois, Iowa, Kansas, Maine, Maryland, Massachusetts, Mississippi, Missouri, Nebraska, New Hampshire, New Jersey, Puerto Rico, Utah, Vermont, West Virginia[141]

---

age that inevitably result when staff is temporarily diverted from one place to another."[142]

Pointer: Success in a work-stoppage state may hinge on the scope of operations that the UI agency evaluates. If you are striking all the employer's facilities in the state, and some are shut down while others are open, ask the agency to look at each facility separately. If you are striking one facility out of many, urge the agency to evaluate the entire operation.

Permanent replacement. Most UI programs grant eligibility if an employer notifies a striker that he or she has been permanently replaced. Some award benefits if a business hires a full complement of new workers—even if the employer does not inform individual strikers of their replacement.[143]

Token offers. A union may be able to establish UI eligibility by extending a return-to-work offer, even though the strike continues. One circumstance is where the employer unilaterally implements its final offer before or during the strike. If the union submits an offer to return "under the terms of the expired agreement," it can expect the employer to refuse, as is its right when the union's offer is conditional. (See Chapter 14.) In some states, this converts the strike into a lockout and qualifies employees for benefits.[144]

Another scenario is an employer that hires a large number of permanent replacements. A return-to-work offer can create UI eligibility for workers not offered reinstatement.[145]

Lockout. Thirty-four states and Puerto Rico (see box on next page) pay UI benefits if an employer locks out employees, even if operations have ceased. Definitions of qualifying lockouts vary. See pages 135–136.

Kentucky and Minnesota treat a work stoppage as a lockout if the employer imposes terms so unreasonable that employees have little alternative but to stop work. In one case, Minnesota awarded UI benefits when an employer provoked a walkout by cutting wages by 26 percent.[146]

Pennsylvania, Ohio, Maryland, Iowa, and West Virginia treat a work stoppage as a lockout if the employer refuses to extend the contract pending further negotiations or refuses to assure the union that the status quo will be maintained pending a new agreement.[147] Connecticut applies a similar rule.

STATES THAT AWARD BENEFITS DURING LOCKOUTS

Arkansas, California (common law), Colorado, Connecticut, Delaware, Florida, Georgia, Illinois, Indiana (common law), Iowa (common law), Kentucky, Louisiana (common law), Maine, Maryland, Massachusetts, Minnesota, Mississippi, Montana (common law), New Hampshire, New Jersey, New York (after eight weeks), Ohio, Oklahoma, Oregon (narrow coverage), Pennsylvania, Puerto Rico, Rhode Island, South Dakota, Tennessee, Texas (common law), Utah (common law), Vermont, Washington, West Virginia, Wisconsin

---

Vacation pay

Employees with scheduled vacations may be able to claim vacation pay during the strike. In some cases, strikers can claim unscheduled days.

Accrued benefits. Under Board rules, an employer must pay accrued vacation benefits during a strike unless it has a justifiable reason for suspending payments based on contract language, benefit plan descriptions, or past practice.[148] Benefits are accrued if they are earned by prior service and are currently due and payable. If the employer refuses to pay, the union can file charges at the NLRB or take the matter to arbitration.[149]

Defenses. Employers sometimes argue that a vacation is a break from work and that since strikers are not working they cannot qualify. This argument breaks down if the employer has a practice of paying vacation benefits during medical, union, or industrial accident leaves, or when employees work through their vacation periods.

Some contracts require that employees work the day before their vacation begins. In that case, employees can only qualify if their vacations are scheduled the first day of the strike.

Request. When asking for vacation pay, strikers should state their intentions to take a vacation.

Date: April 2, 2006
To: Labor Relations Department
From: A.F. Richardson
Re: Vacation

This is to notify you that I will be taking my vacation from April 8 through April 22 of this year, as scheduled. Please send my vacation pay to my home.

Disability pay

Disability pay is generally considered an accrued benefit. Accordingly, workers disabled prior to a strike are normally entitled to continued benefits, including, where it is part of the disability plan, health insurance.[150]

Some disability plans suspend benefits during strikes. For example, a plan may require that an employee be disabled from taking part in "scheduled work." If the facility is no longer operating, no such work exists. An employer may not cancel disability benefits simply because an employee appears on a picket line.[151]

QUESTIONS & ANSWERS

TRI-STATE WORKFORCE

Q. Union members live in three states. When it comes to determining their eligibility to collect unemployment insurance, which UI law applies —the state where the employee lives or the state where the employer's facility is located?

A. Although employees may file in their own state, eligibility is determined by the law of the state where the employer is located.

HOLIDAY PAY

Q. If we go out on strike on July 3, will the employer have to pay holiday pay for July 4?

A. This depends. Holiday pay is normally an accrued benefit.[152] But if the expired contract required employees to work the day before the holiday, payments will not be due.

FOOD STAMPS

Q. Can strikers qualify for food stamps?

A. Perhaps. The food stamp program excludes strikers unless the striker was eligible before the strike. But the exclusion does not apply if the striker is pregnant, over age 60, or must care for a child less than six years of age. Nor are workers excluded if they have been permanently replaced or locked out.

WORKERS' COMPENSATION

Q. Will employees on workers' compensation before the strike continue to receive payments?

A. Yes, if they remain disabled.

PENALTIES

Q. What penalties can a health plan incur if the administrator fails to notify a striker of his or her COBRA rights?

A. First, the plan is subject to a penalty of $110 per day, payable to the employee. Second, the U.S. Department of Labor can conduct an audit. Third, the IRS can impose an excise tax of $100 per day. Fourth, the striker can sue to recover health benefits lost because of the violation.

KEY-MAN STRIKE

Q. If we strike one department, and this forces the company to lay off others in the union, could the laid-off employees collect UI?

A. No. UI programs disqualify employees who are laid off due to a strike by fellow bargaining unit members.

TEMPORARY JOB

Q. If a striker takes a three-week job from another employer during the strike, could he collect UI benefits when the job ends?

A. Probably not. Many states disqualify strikers despite new employment. In others, the striker must work 15 or more weeks for a new employer.

RESUMING PRODUCTION

Q. We signed a contract at the end of our strike but the company only called back half the workforce because of lost customers. Are the unreinstated workers entitled to UI benefits?

A. This depends. Most state UI programs grant benefits when an employer fails to call back workers at the end of a strike. But a work-stoppage state may disqualify if the the loss of business was caused by the strike.

CLOSURE

Q. If a company closes for good during a strike, can workers collect UI benefits?

A. Probably yes. Even work-stoppage states award benefits when an employer permanently shuts its doors.

Chapter 11

Wages of Sin

The rattlesnake, the toad, and the vampire • Pay and benefits •
Fining deserters • Anti-strikebreaker laws • De-unionization

In the summer of 1981, President Ronald Reagan broke an air traffic controllers' strike by bringing in 11,000 strikebreakers. In the years since, employers have been more aggressive in hiring replacement workers, even when goon squads are needed to shepherd them through the gates.

The rattlesnake, the toad, and the vampire

Strikebreakers can be grouped into three categories:

- Workers hired during the strike or transferred from other jobs or facilities (replacements)
- Bargaining unit members who refuse to join (nonstrikers)
- Bargaining unit members who return to work (crossovers)

Trade unionists revile strikebreakers of all stripes, frequently quoting a description by author Jack London:

The Scab

After God had finished the rattlesnake, the toad, and the vampire, He had some awful substance left with which he made a "SCAB."

A SCAB is a two-legged animal with a corkscrew soul, a water-logged brain, and a combination backbone of jelly and glue. Where others have hearts, he carries a tumor of rotten principles.

When a SCAB comes down the street, men turn their backs, angels weep in heaven, and the devil shuts the gates of hell to keep him out.

No man has a right to SCAB so long as there is a pool of water deep enough to drown his body in, or a rope long enough to hang his carcass with. Judas Iscariot was a gentleman compared with a SCAB. For betraying his master, he had character enough to hang himself. A SCAB has not.

Esau sold his birthright for a mess of pottage. Judas sold his Savior for thirty pieces of silver. Benedict Arnold sold his country for a promise of a commission in the British army. The modern strikebreaker sells his birthright, his country, his wife, his children, and his fellowmen for an unfulfilled promise from his employer, trust, or corporation.

Esau was a traitor to himself. Judas was a traitor to his God. Benedict Arnold was a traitor to his country. A SCAB is a traitor to his God, his country, his family, and his class.

Pay and benefits

The NLRA affords employers considerable freedom to hire strikebreakers and to set their terms of employment.

Hiring. A struck employer may bring in replacement workers as soon as the strike begins. If the strike is economic (see Chapter 13), the employer can hire on either a temporary or a permanent basis. If the walkout is a ULP strike, the employer may only hire on a temporary basis. There is no obligation to notify the union.

Pay and benefits. An employer can set the pay, benefits, and working conditions of replacement workers without discussion with the union and without reference to the expired bargaining agreement. The employer can pay reduced wages, deny benefits, and disregard job qualification requirements.

The one thing an employer may not do freely is to pay strikebreakers more than what it has offered the union at the bargaining table. For example, if the starting wage for a welder is $10.00 an hour under the expired contract, and the employer's best offer to the union is a two percent increase, the most the employer can offer a replacement is $10.20 an hour. A higher rate, without a legitimate business justification, is a ULP because it discriminates against the bargaining unit.[153] An exception may apply if the employer is unable to recruit replacements at the final-offer rate.

Information request. A striking union can request the names and addresses of replacement workers, their positions and wages, whether they are temporary or permanent, and the names of the strikers they are replacing.[154]

The employer can withhold names and addresses if union-sponsored threats or violence creates a "clear and present danger" that the union will use the information to harass replacements.[155] This does not excuse the employer from providing job titles, pay rates, and the names of replaced strikers. Refusing an information request risks converting a strike to ULP status.

Nonstrikers and crossovers. The wages and benefits of bargaining unit members who stay on the job remain subject to the expired contract. Any changes must be negotiated with the union, with the possible exception of a change that is expressly limited to the period of the strike.[156]

Offering a raise, bonus, or promotion to entice a striker to return is illegal.[157] So is offering extra pay for the alleged risks involved in crossing a picket line.[158]

Seniority. An employer may not grant line crossers extra service credits that would give them higher seniority than strikers with more service time.[159] If nonstrikers or crossovers are credited with service credits during the strike, the employer must credit an equal amount of time to returning strikers.[160]

REQUEST FOR INFORMATION

Date: July 26, 2006
To: Vince Moffet, Labor Relations Director
From: Toby Guardia, President, Local 44
Re: Request for information

To verify that you are paying replacement workers and nonstrikers no more than your last offer to the union, and to help in formulating bargaining proposals, the union requests the following information:

• The names and addresses of all employees performing bargaining unit work

• Each such employee's current position, date of hire, starting wage rate, and current wage rate

• For replacements, whether the replacement is temporary or permanent

• For permanent replacements, the name of the employee whose position the replacement is taking

The union assures that it will share information about replacements only with the union leadership and the union attorney, and will not use it for the purposes of harassment or intimidation.

Fining deserters

Union constitutions generally allow locals to fine or expel members who refuse to join an authorized strike, return before it is over, or refuse to picket. The union must serve charges and hold a hearing.

The union can enforce a fine in court if the amount is reasonable. For strikebreaking, a reasonable sum is wages earned plus administrative costs.[161]

Resignations. A member who resigns from the union before returning to work cannot be fined. Consequently, union constitutions often forbid resignations during a strike. But in a 1985 case called *Pattern Makers*, the Supreme Court said that anti-resignation rules are unenforceable.[162]

The NLRB has ruled against bylaws that delay the effective date of resignations or impose other procedural barriers. Agreements among strikers to pay each other a cash penalty if they desert have also been invalidated.[163] About the only rule a union can enforce is that resignations be in writing.[164]

Future work. Resignation or expulsion from the union does not prevent a scab from continuing to work when the strike concludes. If the new contract contains a union-security clause, the scab can satisfy it by tendering a weekly or monthly amount equal to dues. The union may not impose a new initiation fee unless the scab asks to rejoin. Telling members that they will lose their jobs if they resign or are expelled is unlawful.

Anti-strikebreaker laws

Laws in many states bar the hiring of strike replacements but unfortunately have little practical value; a constitutional doctrine called "preemption" prevents the enforcement of state laws that conflict with the NLRA. The following are typical of laws that have been struck down under the preemption doctrine:

• No hiring of permanent replacements during a strike (Minnesota)
• No hiring of persons who customarily or repeatedly offer themselves for employment during strikes (Michigan)
• No recruitment or hiring by outside businesses for struck firms (Ohio)

Advertisements. Laws that require advertisements for replacement workers to mention the existence of a strike have received a mixed reception in the courts.[165]

De-unionization

With permanent replacements or crossovers on board, the employer may go the final yard and try to de-unionize.

Withdrawal of recognition. Under NLRA rules, an employer may withdraw union recognition if it has objective proof— for example, individual statements or a signed disaffection petition — that half or more of the bargaining unit no longer wants to be represented. For the first 12 months after a strike begins, the bargaining unit for determining representation consists of strikers, crossovers, nonstrikers, and permanent replacements.

Example: Local 21 struck on April 1. All 40 workers in the bargaining unit joined the walkout. Over the next two weeks, the company hired 40 permanent replacements. On April 15, the replacements circulated a petition declaring that they did not want representation by Local 21 or any other union. Each of the 40 replacements signed. On April 18, the company withdrew recognition because the petition was signed by 50 percent of the 80-worker bargaining unit.

A union can challenge withdrawal by contending that the employer pressured employees to sign a petition or to disclaim support for the union; that employer ULPs caused disaffection with the union; that the replacements were not hired on a permanent basis; that the unit is larger than what the employer claims; or that the employer hired more replacements than necessary to create the basis for de-unionization.

After the strike's one-year anniversary, the bargaining unit for representational purposes no longer includes permanently replaced strikers.[166] This enables the employer to withdraw recognition with fewer supporters.

Example: On May 1, 2005, 60 workers at radio station WRIX went on strike. Over the next year, the station hired 32 permanent replacements. On May 1, 2006, all of the replacements signed a disaffection petition. As the bargaining unit now only numbers 60 (the 32 replacements and the 28 nonreplaced strikers), the employer can withdraw recognition.

Decertification election. Another method to de-unionize is an election. The NLRB will conduct a decertification vote if a unit employee submits a disaffection petition signed by 30% of the bargaining unit. Management cannot collect signatures, but it can provide information on NLRB procedures. An employer can petition for

a decertification election itself if it has objective evidence that the union has lost its majority status.

If the decertification election is held within 12 months of the strike's commencement, eligible voters will include replaced strikers, nonreplaced strikers, crossovers, nonstrikers, and permanent replacements. The only strikers who will not be able to vote are those who have taken equivalent employment elsewhere with no intent to return and those whose positions have been eliminated for legitimate economic reasons.

A striker who takes a job elsewhere can preserve her right to vote in a decertification election by continuing to picket or by notifying the employer that she intends to return when the strike is over.[167]

If a decertification election is held more than 12 months after the strike's commencement, the only eligible voters will be crossovers, nonstrikers, permanent replacements, and nonreplaced strikers. Permanently replaced strikers no longer have a franchise.

RESIGNATION BY MAIL

Q. A member put his resignation in the mail Wednesday afternoon and crossed the picket line Thursday morning. The union received the resignation Friday. Can we fine the bastard?

A. This depends. Under NLRB rules, a mailed resignation takes effect at 12:01 a.m. on the day after its postmark.[168] If the letter is postmarked Wednesday, the union is out of luck. If Thursday, you can impose a fine.

EMPLOYER ASSISTANCE

Q. The president of the company is advising crossovers to resign from the union to avoid being fined and is providing sample resignation letters. Is this allowed?

A. Yes, if the union has threatened to impose fines.

SUPERVISOR MEMBERS

Q. Can we fine a supervisor-member who worked during the strike?

A. Yes, if he performed rank-and-file duties.

JOB SECURITY

Q. The company told a striker with six months of seniority that if she came back to work, she could take a position that is reserved for workers with more than 20 years of service. Can we warn her that she could lose the position when the strike ends?

A. Yes. The union may be able to settle the strike with an agreement that strikers return to their regular positions. Another scenario: the strike is a ULP strike, the union offers to return, and the NLRB orders strikers reinstated to their original positions.

REPLACEMENT PROCEDURE

Q. In the second week of the strike, management notified five employees with the highest pay in the unit that they were replaced. Didn't the company have to follow the layoff clause in the expired contract and replace junior workers first?

A. Not necessarily. The company must continue to honor the expired contract. But if the layoff clause does not mention strikes, there was no discussion of strike replacements when the parties negotiated it, and there is no past practice of replacing strikers by seniority, the Board is unlikely to rule that the clause controls replacement decisions.

BYRNES ACT

Q. Doesn't the Byrnes Act forbid the hiring of strikebreakers?

A. No. The Byrnes Act, a 1936 federal law, forbids an employer from transporting scabs across state lines for the purpose of using "force or threats" against peaceful union picketing. The law may apply to armed goons, but not to run-of-the-mill strikebreakers.[169]

UNDERCOVER AGENTS

Q. Our employer is advertising for strike replacements. Can we send in applicants?

A. Yes. Sending in surreptitious applicants is called "salting." The salt—usually a friend, relative, or a member of a sister union—may discover illegal wage offers or other evidence that can convert the strike to ULP status. The salt may also be able to testify that the employer did not promise permanent employment.

An employer may not reject a strike applicant because he or she is a union member or is related to a striker. It can, however, refuse to hire a paid union staff member.[170]

Chapter 12

Discharges

Discharge rules • ULP charges • Grievances • Arbitration

Bosses count on firings to intimidate and demoralize the bargaining unit. But workers often respond with a stronger determination to stay the course. A discharge that lacks sufficient grounds can turn an economic strike into a ULP strike and annul the employer's right to hire permanent replacements.

Discharge rules

An employer may not discharge, discipline, or deny a striker reinstatement unless the striker committed "egregious misconduct."[171] Firing a striker for a minor offense, such as insubordination or name-calling, is an unfair labor practice.

New standard. Prior to 1984, the NLRB narrowly defined egregious misconduct. Although it sustained discharges when strikers engaged in assaults, property destruction, and extensive blocking, it often excused interference with line crossers as "strike exuberance" and verbal threats as "strike rhetoric."

In *Clear Pine Mouldings*, the Board expanded the notion of egregious misconduct to include actions or threats that are "reasonably likely" to coerce or intimidate a nonstriker from crossing a picket line.[172] *Clear Pine* allows an employer to fire a striker even if no person complains.

Hit list. Under the *Clear Pine* standard, a striker risks being fired if he or she:

- Warns a line crosser: "You keep doing this, you're going to get your head busted."
- Tells a line crosser: "We know where you live and we're coming to get you."
- Throws a rock, bottle, or other object
- Spits on a line crosser
- Hits a line crosser's vehicle with a picket sign, kicks or rocks it, beats on a hood, or bangs on a window
- Assaults a security guard
- Displays a gun, knife, pipe, slingshot, or other weapon
- Places nails on a road or driveway
- Throws a firecracker
- Builds a physical barrier or forms a human wall
- Tailgates or swerves in front of a line crosser's vehicle

Note: A purely reflexive action is not a dischargeable offense.[173] Nor is common banter such as, "We're going to kick your ass."[174]

Profanity. Employers sometimes claim that *Clear Pine* allows them to fire strikers for yelling "scab" or "asshole." But the Board has not gone quite that far. Absent a threat of violence, a striker may not be cashiered for profanity or obscene gestures, even if the employer has a zero-tolerance harassment policy.[175] The Board has reinstated strikers fired for epithets such as "stupid fucker," "whore," "dickhead," and "motherfucker."[176]

The Board may sustain a discharge, however, if a striker engages in extensive sexual ridicule, profanity carried to abusive levels, taunting for being gay or lesbian, or profanity directed at a customer.

Blocking. Blocking vehicles on a single occasion, or causing minor traffic delays, generally does not justify discipline. Strikers have a right to approach vehicles, attempt to speak with drivers, and hand out literature.[177] But blocking access on several occasions, or for an extended period of time, risks discharge.[178]

Arrests. An employer cannot discharge simply because a striker is arrested or convicted for a picket line offense such as trespass, disorderly conduct, or scuffling with police.[179] The employer must evaluate the coercive impact, if any, on nonstrikers.

Balancing. Historically, the NLRB has been more tolerant of misconduct by ULP strikers than by economic strikers. This is known as the "*Thayer* doctrine." The doctrine has fallen out of favor at the Board but it appears to retain life in the courts.[180]

ULP charges

The union should file a ULP charge if a striker is fired or refused reinstatement. For tactical reasons, it is sometimes better to first file a grievance and a request for information (see pointer on page 110).

Contents. The charge should allege violations of Sections 8(a)(1), (3) and (5) of the NLRA and assert that the infraction has prolonged the strike.

ULP CHARGE

1. On March 24, 2006, the employer fired striker Hans Vogel because of activity on the picket line.

2. On March 25, 2006, the union grieved the discharge. The employer has refused to discuss the grievance.

3. On March 25, 2006, the union requested information relating to Mr. Vogel's discharge. The employer has not responded.

4. The employer's illegal actions have prolonged the strike.

Evidence. Proof of any of the following contentions warrants a Regional Director complaint and a Board decision awarding reinstatement and back pay:

- The striker did not take part in the acts charged.
- The employer acted on impulse or speculation without concrete evidence.
- If there was misconduct, it was not serious.
- The employer punished the striker because he is a picket captain, officer, or other union leader.
- The employer did not fire nonstrikers who committed similarly egregious misconduct.

Double standards. Evidence of unpunished misconduct by strikebreakers, guards, or supervisors creates a strong argument to overturn a firing. As the Board has explained, an employer "may not knowingly tolerate behavior by nonstrikers or replacements that is at least as serious as, or more serious than, [the] conduct of strikers that the employer is relying on to deny reinstatement to jobs."[181]

> **Example:** Hellman Textiles fired James Mason for threatening to burn down a scab's house. Ordinarily this would warrant termination, but a union witness testified that a few days earlier an armed security guard told a striker that he would "blow him away." Because the guard's threat was comparable to the striker's, and because the company only gave the guard a verbal warning, Mason has a strong NLRB case.

Double standards can only be alleged when management is aware of a nonstriker's misconduct. Sending incident notices can protect wayward strikers.

INCIDENT NOTICE

Date: January 5, 2006
To: Tom Smooty, Director of Human Relations
From: Marcia Postal, President, Local 80
Re: Assault

This is to inform you that yesterday, January 4, 2006, at the East Gate, supervisor Rick Smith assaulted striker Timothy Wolf by driving his car directly toward Wolf and swerving at the last instant.

Back pay. When the Board rules in favor of a discharged striker, its standard remedy is reinstatement with back pay from the date of termination— even if this was weeks or months before the strike ended.[182]

Grievances

A struck employer must bargain on grievances during the strike, including the discipline of strikers. It must also supply relevant information. A refusal to meet or to furnish information can convert a strike to ULP status, even if the discipline turns out to be lawful.[183]

Information request. To investigate a disciplinary grievance, the union can ask for incident reports, logbooks, names of witnesses, films, and personnel files.

> **Note:** Under Board policy, an employer can withhold the written or recorded statements of witnesses, including line crossers and security guards. An employer that invokes this privilege must offer to supply the union with summaries.[184]

INFORMATION REQUEST

Date: October 5, 2006
To: Emily Peabody, Director of Labor Relations
From: Howard Mintz, Business Agent, Local 22
Re: Discharge of striker Jim Penny

The union requests the following information to help it investigate the Jim Penny grievance:

a. A copy of Penny's personnel file

b. A full description of his alleged misconduct

c. The names of all witnesses to the alleged misconduct

d. All investigative records and reports concerning the alleged misconduct

e. Copies of all incident reports and other documents referring or relating to misconduct by nonstriking employees from the first day of the strike

f. The disciplinary and personnel files of the following supervisors, replacement workers, and crossovers who have engaged in strike misconduct: Brad Richards, Sue Williams, and Ken Greeb

---

Pointer: A union can lose its rights to information if, at the time of its request, it has filed a ULP charge concerning the underlying dispute.[185] The employer can also refuse to meet and bargain.[186] This suggests the following schedule: First, file a grievance contending that the discharge lacks just cause. Second, request a meeting. Third, submit a request for information. Fourth, wait two weeks. Fifth, file a ULP charge alleging that the discharge, the failure to provide information, and the failure to meet violate the NLRA.

Arbitration

Since no contract is in place, a union cannot arbitrate discharges during a strike. But it is common to agree on this procedure as part of a strike settlement.

Arbitrator versus ALJ. For several reasons, a union will generally have a better chance of winning reinstatement from a labor arbitrator than an NLRB judge (ALJ):

- Arbitrators normally allow unions to argue disparate treatment within the bargaining unit.
- Arbitrators normally take into account mitigating factors such as length of service.
- An arbitrator can reduce a discharge to a suspension, an option unavailable to an ALJ.
- An employer can only appeal an arbitrator's decision to the courts on narrow grounds; ALJ decisions can more easily be appealed.

On the flip side:

- An employee who wins before an ALJ can expect back pay from the date of discharge; an arbitrator is more likely to order wages from the date the strike ended.
- An employer may insist that the arbitrator's authority be limited to a determination of whether the striker committed the acts charged; an ALJ will hear all issues recognized by Board law.

QUESTIONS & ANSWERS

DELAYED ACTION

Q. When the strike ended, the company refused to reinstate four employees because of picket line misconduct. Do we have a case because management failed to act when the incidents occurred?

A. No. An employer can wait until the end of the strike to announce discipline.

SPITTING

Q. Can a company fire a striker for spitting on a scab?

A. Yes. Spitting is a form of assault.[187]

BACK PAY

Q. If the NLRB rules that a striker was wrongfully discharged, does it always award full back pay?

A. No. The pay award will be reduced if the striker made no attempts to find work, had earnings since the discharge, or admits that if he had not been fired he would have remained out of work for the remainder of the strike. Moreover, if the striker was permanently replaced prior to his discharge, his right to back pay may be contingent on the departure of the employee who replaced him.[188]

Chapter 13

Name that Strike

*Categories • Reinstatement rights • ULP strategy •
Identifying pre-strike ULPs • Identifying mid-strike ULPs •
Positioning the strike • Reconversion • Illegal strikes*

U nder the NLRA, a work stoppage is either an economic strike or an unfair-labor-practice (ULP) strike. A strike's classification takes on particular importance with the following sequence of events:

1. The employer hires permanent replacements.
2. The union unconditionally offers to return to work.
3. Because the replacements are occupying jobs, the employer has insufficient vacancies to reinstate strikers who want to return.

Although this scenario plays out in only a small minority of strikes, projections about a walkout's legal character frequently affect decision-making by employers, unions, and strikers.

Categories

The terms "economic strike" and "ULP strike" refer to the issues that caused or prolonged the stoppage.

Economic strike. A strike undertaken solely to obtain movement in collective bargaining or to win union recognition is an economic strike.

ULP strike. A strike caused or prolonged by employer conduct that violates the National Labor Relations Act (NLRA) is a ULP strike. Although a ULP violation must be a precipitating factor, it need not be the sole or even the major reason behind the walkout. Nor must the union disclaim a contract objective.

> **Example:** Local 10's overriding contract goal was an improved wage scale. At the third bargaining session, the company's lead negotiator said that the company could not afford the union's demands. To verify the truth of the matter, the union asked to see the company's books, including its profit and loss statements. Despite its legal obligation to supply the information, the company ignored the request. Angered, workers voted to walk out. Although the information refusal was not the only reason for the strike, the walkout is a ULP strike.[189]

Conversion. Some work stoppages are ULP strikes from the first day. Others begin as economic disputes but change when a ULP injects new issues into bargaining or hardens strikers' resolve to stay out. When an economic strike is prolonged or aggravated by illegal employer conduct, the strike "converts" to ULP status.

> **Example:** Local 5 hit the bricks for economic reasons. In the second week, five strikers were discharged for picketing the owner's home. Because the illegal discharges added a contentious issue to the bargaining table, and delayed settlement, the strike converted to ULP status.

Reinstatement rights

Most strikes, even those in which the employer hires permanent replacements, end with a new contract and an agreement to reinstate strikers. A strong union may have sufficient leverage to force the employer to dismiss replacement workers. A union with less leverage may have to allow the replacements to remain, with displaced strikers put on a preferential recall list.

A union that is unable to negotiate a satisfactory settlement can submit an "unconditional offer to return." The offer may reflect a Trojan Horse strategy to move the struggle inside (see next chapter), or may simply be an attempt to avoid decertification. In any case, unless the parties execute a back-to-work accord, the union's post-offer reinstatement rights will rest on the strike's legal status.

Economic strike. In both an economic and a ULP strike, an employer has two choices after a union's unconditional offer to return: accept the offer or declare a lockout. If the employer accepts the offer, and the strike is economic, it must set a prompt return date and dismiss any temporary replacements holding strikers' jobs. But it may allow permanent replacements and crossovers to retain the jobs they held during the conflict. Unreinstated strikers must be placed on a preferential recall ("Laidlaw") list to await the appearance of vacancies or the creation of new positions.

ULP strike. If the walkout is a ULP strike, and the employer does not declare a lockout, the employer must reinstate all strikers to their former positions—even if this requires the dismissal of permanent strike replacements.[190] Failure to reinstate starts strikers' back pay clocks.

> **Example:** When BK Plastics failed to bargain in good faith, 100 workers went on strike. Over the next month, the company hired a complete complement of permanent replacements. Realizing they had lost the strike, the union submitted an unconditional return-to-work offer. The employer, claiming that the strike was economic, put the strikers on a Laidlaw list. The union filed ULP charges, continued to picket, and told members to apply for unemployment insurance.
>
> Six months later, an ALJ ruled that because the walkout was a ULP strike, the company had to reinstate the strikers and pay them back wages from the date the union offered to return.

Converted strike. When a strike converts to ULP status, the rights of strikers depend on the conversion date. The employer can retain replacements hired before conversion, even if this prevents strikers from returning.

> **Example:** On January 9, 80 Giant Motors workers struck for a new contract. On January 10, the company hired 20 permanent replacements. On January 12, the company fired three strikers, converting the walkout to ULP status. On January 25, the company hired 60 more replacements.
>
> If the union offers to return on January 26, how many strikers will be entitled to immediate reinstatement? The answer is 60, because the com-

pany does not have to dismiss the 20 replacements hired before the strike's conversion date.

Note: An employer can reconvert a ULP strike to an economic one. Replacements hired after the reconversion date can be retained at the expense of returning strikers. (See page 121.)

ULP strategy

A ULP strategy consists of identifying ULPs, filing NLRB charges, and positioning a strike around the infractions. The strategy does not guarantee that the employer will follow the law and restrict hiring to temporaries. Nor does it guarantee that the employer will discharge permanent replacements when the strike is over. Employers frequently ignore the rules, knowing that it may take years before the NLRB orders strikers reinstated. Nonetheless, a ULP strategy has several advantages for a striking union:

• The employer may hold back from hiring permanent replacements because of the possibility that a Board order will force it to reinstate strikers with back wages.

• Strikers will be less likely to panic if the employer hires permanent replacements, knowing that if the strike fails there is a way to force the employer to take them back.

• The NLRB may refuse to process a decertification petition or to allow the employer to withdraw recognition.

Waiting to strike. Savvy employers avoid ULPs by going through the proper bargaining motions, answering information requests, and refraining from illegal threats. In that event, the union may want to conduct an aggressive inside campaign. (See Chapter 2.) Job protests frequently provoke unfair labor practices.

Example: During bargaining for a new agreement, Kary's Foods gave the union no grounds to file ULP charges. When the contract expired, the union stayed on the job and commenced off-duty picketing. Angered, the company filmed the pickets and issued warnings for disloyalty. These infractions enabled the union to call a ULP strike.

Note: The NLRB is more likely to classify a stoppage as a ULP strike if the ULPs are near in time to the strike's inception. But this is not an absolute requirement; the Board has awarded ULP status to strikes that protested ULPs that occurred months earlier.[191]

Identifying pre-strike ULPs

The most common pre-strike ULPs are:

- Bad-faith bargaining
- Refusal to supply relevant bargaining information
- Insistence on permissive or illegal bargaining subjects
- Unilateral changes
- Threats

Bad-faith bargaining. Bad-faith bargaining can be defined as negotiating without being open to compromise or with no intention of coming to an agreement. Typical characteristics are cancelled meetings, unreasonable proposals, unilateral changes, a take-it-or-leave-it posture, withdrawal of agreed-upon provisions, and giving negotiators insufficient authority.

Refusing to negotiate on working conditions or benefits unless the union first accepts the employer's wage proposal is bad-faith bargaining.[192] So is refusing to discuss wages until the union agrees to the employer's position on noneconomic matters.[193] Insisting on proposals that would prevent the union from representing its members is also illegal.[194]

Unions know that bad-faith bargaining takes place in many negotiations. But the NLRB takes a parsimonious approach, often labeling outrageous employer behavior as "hard bargaining."

Failure to furnish information. An employer commits a ULP if it fails to comply with a union request for documents or data relevant to negotiations. The union can request information about pension contributions, insurance plans, subcontracting, and other subjects, and can demand internal studies, correspondence, and contracts.

If an employer claims that benefits in its other branches or divisions are lower than in the bargaining unit, demand the benefit plans and collective-bargaining agreements covering these entities.[195] If the employer is asking for increases in health care contributions, ask for information on claims submitted by unit and non-unit plan participants and the premiums paid on their behalf.[196]

If the employer asserts that it is "losing money," is in "bad shape," or "cannot afford" union terms, demand financial data, including profit-and-loss reports.[197]

Insistence on permissive or illegal bargaining subjects. The NLRA recognizes three categories of bargaining subjects: mandatory, permissive, and illegal. Mandatory subjects relate directly to wages, benefits, or working conditions. Permissive subjects include extraneous matters and union prerogatives. Illegal subjects directly conflict with NLRA provisions or rules.

An employer may propose language on a permissive or illegal subject, and may even ask for it repeatedly. But it commits a ULP if it announces that the contract must include the proposal, if it makes acquiescence a condition for further bargaining, or if its insistence creates a bargaining impasse.

Permissive subjects include demands that the union:

- Give up bargaining unit classifications
- Change a multi-plant bargaining unit to separate units
- Withdraw or agree not to file a ULP charge, grievance, or lawsuit

- Pay for property damage
- Agree to a grievance procedure that allows the employer to adjust grievances without the presence of the union
- Agree to a "loyalty" clause obligating employees to protect employer interests
- Accept the assistance of a government mediator
- Allow the employer to negotiate wages with individual employees
- Agree to an "Evergreen clause" under which the contract would continue after its expiration date until the parties execute a new agreement
- Afford superseniority to strike replacements or non-strikers
- Agree to a strike settlement forbidding the union from imposing discipline against members who scabbed during the strike
- Limit the period of a Laidlaw list
- Reveal the names of employees who committed property damage or other strike misconduct

Unilateral changes. An employer commits a ULP if it implements part or all of its final offer, or makes other significant changes, before reaching a bonafide impasse on the contract as a whole. Work rules and benefit reductions are common infractions.

A bona fide impasse occurs when the employer and the union are at a deadlock with no realistic prospects that further discussions will be fruitful. An employer may not declare impasse before the parties have completed bargaining on all mandatory subjects or while union information requests are pending on issues separating the parties.

To prevent or delay impasse, union negotiators should:
- Submit counterproposals
- Never say that negotiations are deadlocked—not even to members
- Never use terms such as "final," "deal-breaker," or "never"
- Always assert the union's willingness to compromise
- Delay mediation
- Always have an information request pending
- Never leave a meeting without attempting to schedule another

- Postpone meetings when union representatives are legitimately busy with other matters

Threats. An employer can warn employees that they risk permanent replacement if they take part in an economic strike. But because replaced workers have preferential reinstatement rights, a threat that workers will "lose their jobs" or "never come back" is a ULP. So is a threat to close the company or move equipment to other facilities.[198]

Surveillance, warnings, or discipline directed against workers who take part in inside activities can also create the basis for a ULP strike.[199]

Identifying mid-strike ULPs

An economic strike converts to a ULP strike if the employer commits a violation that prolongs the conflict. Common infractions include:
- Refusing to meet or bargain
- Discharging strikers without adequate grounds
- Causing strikers to be wrongly arrested
- Refusing to discuss grievances or to supply information
- Violence or threats of violence
- Videotaping peaceful picketing or rallies
- Direct dealing
- Refusing to pay accrued benefits
- Paying replacement workers at rates higher than those offered to the union
- Granting superseniority to nonstrikers or scab replacements

For other examples, see list on pages 46–47.

Refusal to bargain. The employer must continue to bargain during the strike unless the union engages in flagrant violence.

Discharges. It is illegal to fire a striker for a minor infraction or for conduct that is tolerated from nonstrikers. (See Chapter 12.) Unlawful discharges lead "inexorably to the prolongation of a dispute."[200]

Refusal to hear grievances. An employer must bargain over discipline and other grievances during a strike. It must also supply relevant information such as investigative reports, films, and the records of nonstrikers who committed similar misconduct.

Videotaping. Photographing or videotaping orderly strike activity is a ULP unless the employer had a reasonable basis to anticipate violence or other unlawful conduct.

Violence. Assaults by supervisors are ULPs. Examples: driving dangerously close to a picket line; pushing a striker to the ground; brandishing a weapon.

Positioning the strike

Filing a meritorious ULP charge does not guarantee that a strike will be awarded ULP status. The union must also establish that the unlawful conduct touched off the work stoppage or extended it. Several measures can be taken to bolster this contention.

Inform the membership. Discuss the ULP in meetings, newsletters, and rallies. Post ULP charges in the union hall.

If the union holds a strike vote, read the ULP charge and enter the discussion in the minutes. Phrase the vote to emphasize the violation:

> Does the membership agree to strike because the employer has violated the NLRA by making unilateral changes and because it has refused to negotiate a fair collective bargaining agreement?

If ULPs occur during the strike, pass a resolution condemning them or take a new vote along the following lines:

> Do the members agree that in view of the employer's illegal activities, they shall continue the strike?

Inform the employer. Notify the employer that the union considers itself to be on a ULP strike and use the term in correspondence. Add a remedy for the ULP to the union's list of bargaining demands and maintain the demand until the strike concludes.

Inform the press and the public. Issue a press release describing the walkout as a ULP strike and cite the ULP when giving interviews to the media and in union literature. Refer to the violation on your picket signs. Examples: "On strike against bad-faith bargaining" or "On strike because of discriminatory treatment."

Push the NLRB. When filing ULP charges prior to a strike, inform the Region that the union may strike over the matter. If the strike has already begun, allege that the ULP caused or is prolonging the walkout. The NLRB Casehandling Manual instructs investigators to consider connections between ULPs and strikes and, where appropriate, to include a ULP-strike allegation when issuing a complaint.[201]

ULP CHARGE

1. On August 1, 2006, the employer videotaped peaceful union picketing.

2. On August 4, 2006, a supervisor threatened a striker that the plant would close.

3. On August 6, 2006, a supervisor purposely drove into the picket line.

4. The above ULP violations have prolonged the strike currently engaged in by the bargaining unit.

Reconversion

As if the subject was not confusing enough, the Board says an employer can reconvert a ULP strike to economic status if it "cures" its misconduct. Reconversion allows an employer to hire permanent replacements.

Requirements. Although Board law has not been completely consistent, it appears that an employer must "fully remedy" its ULPs to lay a basis for reconversion.[202] This means the employer must:

• Inform the entire bargaining unit that it is rescinding its illegal actions

• Make employees whole for any losses caused by a ULP

• Assure employees that it will not again interfere with their Section 7 rights

NLRB settlement. An employer may try to settle ULP charges to prevent a strike from being awarded ULP status. The NLRB does not need the union's consent to settle. Some unions hold additional charges in a back pocket in case the Region settles out their initial claims.

An NLRB settlement may require the employer to post a Board notice for 60 days. Until the posting period expires, a ULP strike maintains its status.[203] The union can take advantage by offering to return before the 60th day.

Illegal strikes

A strike is illegal if it violates an NLRA provision such as the requirement to serve a 60-day termination notice (see Chapter 1). A strike is also illegal if the union is demanding a contract provision that is barred by the NLRA, such as a clause allowing employees to honor secondary picket lines. When a strike is illegal, the employer can refuse to bargain, can make unilateral changes, and can refuse to reinstate strikers.

Union insistence on a permissive subject. According to the Board, a strike is illegal if the union insists on a permissive subject of bargaining as a condition of signing an agreement.[204] Among the subjects that are considered permissive are demands that an employer:

- Add a classification to the union bargaining unit
- Join a multi-employer bargaining unit
- Place a union label on company products
- Resolve a pending grievance
- Withdraw a lawsuit
- Agree to interest arbitration
- Allow the union to record bargaining sessions
- Give the union a seat on the board of directors
- Agree to refrain from campaigning against union efforts to organize additional bargaining units
- Extend amnesty to strikers who committed strike misconduct
- Fire permanent replacements hired during an economic strike

Pointer: If you settle out all your mandatory subjects, you run the risk of being left with permissive demands holding up a final settlement. Keep at least one mandatory demand on the table to avoid making the strike illegal.

SAFETY STRIKE

Q. Is a strike to protest a dangerous condition, such as an OSHA violation, a ULP strike?

A. No. OSHA infractions or other safety hazards do not violate the NLRA.

ASSURANCES

Q. If we are sure that our strike is a ULP strike, can we promise members that they will not lose their jobs to strikebreakers?

A. No. A ULP strike has advantages over an economic strike, but it does not guarantee that workers will keep their jobs. For example, the employer may hire permanent replacements despite the law. If the strike stalls, the union may decide that its best course is a settlement that allows some replacements to remain.

REPLACEMENT THREAT

Q. We called a ULP strike after the employer implemented its final offer. In the first week, the general manager sent each striker the following letter: "This shall serve as notice that it is the intention of the Whitman Company to permanently replace you unless you report for work within five days." Should we file charges?

A. Yes. Threatening to hire permanent replacements during a ULP strike is illegal, whether the threat is made directly to employees or raised during negotiations with the union.[205]

REGRESSIVE BARGAINING

Q. The employer says that because it has hired strike replacements, it will no longer agree to a union-security clause. Does this convert the strike?

A. No. During an economic strike, an employer can alter its bargaining position to take advantage of a new balance of power.[206]

REINSTATEMENT PROPOSAL

Q. We are trying to negotiate a strike settlement but are hung up on reinstatement. We are insisting that all strikers return to their former positions. The company president says that this is the same as demanding that she fire all the permanent replacements and that she will not discuss the issue. Isn't this bad-faith bargaining?

A. Yes. A proposal that strikers return to their original jobs is a mandatory subject of bargaining.[207]

SCAB LAWSUIT

Q. The labor relations director says that if she dismisses the permanent replacements, they could sue the company for breach of contract. Is she blowing smoke?

A. Hard to say. Courts have ruled that permanent replacements are at-will employees whom the employer can fire for any reason.[208] But this rule does not apply if the employer promises the replacements that they will be secure against a union strike settlement. In that case, the company can avoid liability by obtaining releases from the replacements in return for severance pay.

Chapter 14

Offers to Return

Trojan Horse offer • All-or-none offer

When an employer begins to hire permanent replacements, the union must carefully evaluate its position. If the numbers are small, the union may be able to shrug off the hiring as a scare tactic. But if the employer appears intent on replacing a sizable portion of the bargaining unit, the strike, and indeed the union's future, may be in jeopardy. Three options are:

• Continue the strike, extending it wherever possible

• Accept the employer's final contract offer

• Offer to return to work without a contract

The first choice is high risk. With replacements on board, the employer may refuse to settle without dismantling the seniority and union-security systems. Or it may withdraw recognition or file for a decertification election.

The second option, signing on the employer's terms, may be unthinkable, especially if the employer asks for concessions that decimate long-standing rights and benefits. What about that third idea?

Trojan Horse offer

Other than accepting the employer's contract proposals, the only sure way to defeat a permanent replacement strategy is to submit an unconditional offer to return to work. It is illegal to hire replacements or to award permanent status to temporaries after the offer is received.[209]

Responses. There are only two lawful reactions to a union return-to-work offer: acceptance or lockout. Any other response starts the back-pay clock for each striker entitled to reinstatement.[210]

If the employer accepts the offer, it must set a prompt reporting date for strikers whose positions are vacant or filled by temporaries. (In a ULP strike it must also displace permanent replacements, but this almost always requires NLRB intervention.)

Back on the job, the union can mount a "Trojan Horse" campaign. Employees can wear union insignia, hold rallies, picket before and after shifts, urge customers to boycott, and engage in lawful work-to-rule activities. At the same time the union can try to make life unpleasant for any replacements still working. The inside campaign may be more effective than the strike it succeeds.

If the employer initiates a lockout, either immediately or as a reaction to the union's inside activities, the employer will face several problems:

- It will not be able to hire additional permanent replacements.
- Thirty-four states and Puerto Rico pay UI benefits when workers are locked out (see list on page 92).
- If the employer has committed ULPs—such as making unilateral changes, insisting on nonmandatory bargaining subjects, or refusing to supply the union with relevant information—the NLRB can declare the lockout illegal and order the employer to reinstate workers with back wages. (See pages 134-135.)

Formulating the offer. To bind an employer, a return-to-work offer must not include any conditions or qualifications. An offer to return under "our former terms of employment" is conditional. So is a demand that the employer rectify a ULP or reverse a discharge.

RETURN-TO-WORK OFFER

Date: December 10, 2006
To: Walter Hamilton, President, Northeast Utilities
From: Nora Breakstone, President, Local 20
Re: Return to work

This is to notify the company that Local 20 unconditionally offers to end the strike and return to work immediately. We make this offer for all employees represented by Local 20 and all employees who have honored the picket line.

Please notify the union when workers should report to work.

If the number of returning strikers exceeds the number of available positions, the union requests immediate bargaining on the procedure for filling vacancies.

Picket lines. A union does not have to cease its strike activities while it awaits the employer's response to an offer to return. Nonetheless, to prevent a claim that the offer is bogus, it makes sense to stop picketing for a few days. If the employer rejects the offer, fails to reinstate strikers for whom openings exist, or declares a lockout, the union can resume picketing.

Reinstatement. An employer that accepts a union return-to-work offer must put employees back to work immediately.[211] Delay requires substantial justification, such as a lack of raw materials. The employer may not insist that the union withdraw NLRB charges or sign a return-to-work agreement. Nor may it order strikers to fill out employment applications or to submit to interviews.

Positions. The employer must assign returning strikers to their pre-strike positions or to jobs that are equivalent in terms of salary and duties — if these positions are vacant or occupied by temporary replacements. ULP strikers are entitled to displace permanent replacements.

A striker whose position is not available must be placed on a preferential recall or Laidlaw list. A striker whose position has been eliminated for legitimate business reasons, such as a reorganization of the work, and for whom no equivalent vacancy exists, must also be placed on the list.

The employer can deny reinstatement to a striker who has:

- Taken equivalent employment elsewhere with an intent to leave permanently (not self-employment)
- Resigned or retired (but a resignation solely to obtain vacation or 401K monies does not forfeit job rights)
- Committed serious misconduct

Working conditions. When strikers return to work under an unconditional offer, the employer must resume the wages, benefits, and working conditions in the expired collective bargaining agreement except for changes that the employer has lawfully imposed after a bargaining impasse.[212] Employees may not be forbidden from discussing union matters, distributing union literature, or taking part in lawful protest activities. The employer may not discriminate against or harass the former strikers.

Challenging permanent replacements. A union can challenge the retention of replacement workers by filing ULP charges on the following grounds:

- **The strike was a ULP strike.** As explained above, ULP strikers have an absolute right to return to their original positions, even if this requires the dismissal of workers hired on a permanent basis.

- **The replacements were not hired on a permanent basis.** To qualify a replacement as permanent, the employer and the replacement must have had an understanding, either at the time of hire or later, that the job would continue beyond the strike. Testimony that the employer offered jobs "as long as the strike continues" undercuts the employer's case, as do applications describing employment as "at will."[213] The fact that a strikebreaker is still on probation does not rule out a claim of permanency.

Laidlaw list. The following rules apply to the operation of a Laidlaw list:

- The employer must bargain with the union over how it fills vacancies from the list. The usual method is by department or plant seniority, but a different method can be imposed if the employer bargains to impasse. The method may not discriminate against union activists.

- The employer must offer new or vacant positions to employees on the list before offering them to other employees or hiring from the outside. But the employer does not have to offer a position that is different from the employee's pre-strike job, even if its duties are within the employee's qualifications or experience.[214]

- If the employer offers a former striker a position that is significantly different from his pre-strike job, the striker can decline without jeopardizing his right to stay on the Laidlaw list. If the striker accepts, the employer must offer him a transfer if his pre-strike position or its equivalent opens up in the future.[215]

- The employer must maintain the Laidlaw list until it has offered all former strikers equivalent employment.[216]

The union should file ULP charges if the employer violates a Laidlaw-list rule, hires workers from temporary job agencies, assigns supervisors to perform bargaining unit work, or unnecessarily combines jobs.

All-or-none offer

A Trojan Horse offer is designed for submission just as or before the employer begins to hire permanent replacements. If the union fails to take this path, and large numbers of strikebreakers appear on the scene, an "all-or-none" offer may be the only way to stay in the game.

An all-or-none offer (which can be phrased the same as a Trojan Horse offer) is contingent on the union having grounds for asserting the strike's ULP status. The offer is not submitted with the intention of calling off the strike. Instead, its purpose is (1) to create the basis for an NLRB order reinstating employees with back pay and (2) to qualify strikers for unemployment insurance. Within a few days, the union will declare that it is locked out and resume picketing.

> **Example:** Local 30's 125 members struck Trixie Foods on June 1. Over the next two months, Trixie hired 100 permanent replacements. On August 10, the union submitted an unconditional return-to-work offer. The employer responded by notifying the union that the 25 vacancies would be assigned to the most senior employees and the remaining 100 strikers would be put on a Laidlaw list.
>
> The union filed a ULP charge contending that because the walkout was a ULP strike, all 125 strikers should have been offered reinstatement. The 25 senior workers refused to come back and the 100 employees on the Laidlaw list filed for unemployment benefits.

Back-pay clock. An all-or-none offer starts the back-pay clock for each ULP striker who is not offered immediate reinstatement. If 200 strikers have average wages of $500, the employer's liability will grow at more than $100,000 per week.[217]

Unemployment insurance. In most states, a striker who is not reinstated after an unconditional offer to return qualifies for unemployment insurance (UI) benefits.[218] The payments will be charged to the employer's UI account, increasing pressure to come to terms.

Solidarity. Before making an all-or-none offer, the union should instruct members that anyone offered a job should decline on solidarity grounds. The union can provide a form letter explaining that the worker will return only if the employer fulfills its legal obligation to reinstate all of the ULP strikers. Those who refuse will not be eligible for UI benefits or back pay but will retain their rights to reinstatement if the NLRB finds that the walkout was a ULP strike.[219]

SECRET HIRING

Q. We assumed that the hospital was hiring temporary workers, but now management tells us the replacements are permanent. Did the hospital commit a ULP by sandbagging us?

A. No. Management does not have to give notice to the union before hiring permanent replacements.

RECONNAISSANCE

Q. We are thinking of sending the union vice president back to work to talk to the replacement workers and to check on wages. If the union submits a return offer on his behalf, will the company have to take him back?

A. Yes, if his position or its equivalent is available.

UNION AS AGENT

Q. Can the employer ignore a union offer to return on the grounds that strikers must make individual requests?

A. No. The union speaks for its members.[220]

NO-STRIKE CONDITION

Q. When we submitted an offer to return, the company president said he would only agree if the union pledges not to resume its strike in the future. Is this a lawful requirement?

A. No. An employer may not condition striker reinstatement on a union promise not to resume striking or picketing.[221]

PERMANENT SUBCONTRACT

Q. In response to our return-to-work offer, management said it only had room for two-thirds of the workforce because it had permanently subcontracted most of our duties. Can we file ULP charges?

A. Yes. An employer must have a substantial justification to enter into a long-term or permanent subcontract during a strike, such as an inability to recruit replacements or contractors who would take the work on a temporary basis.[222] Even in this event, the employer must notify the union beforehand and bargain.[223]

Chapter 15

Extreme Games

Lawful lockout • ULP lockout • Partial lockout • UI benefits

For years lockout was a dreaded word in union circles, and the tactic remains a serious threat. But some employers have second thoughts when they learn that they may have to pay for unemployment benefits, cannot hire permanent replacements, and may incur an NLRB back-pay order.

Lawful lockout

A lockout is a temporary withholding of work to affect a labor dispute. In the early years of the NLRA, employers could only use the tactic for defensive reasons, for example, to preempt a sudden walkout that could destroy company products, or to respond to a whipsaw strike. In recent times, the courts and the Board have expanded the permissible grounds.

Under current law, an employer may use a lockout like a union uses a strike: as a tactic to force the other side to sign a contract. The employer can act as soon as the contract expires or during a post-contract inside campaign.[224] An impasse in negotiations is not a prerequisite. Nor is advance notice.

An employer can initiate a lockout when a union tenders an offer to return from a strike. The lockout must be declared immediately and the employer must give a clear and full explanation of the terms with which the union must agree to achieve reinstatement.[225]

ULP lockout

A lockout to force agreement to an employer's contract proposals is only lawful if the employer's bargaining position is "legitimate."[226] If the employer's position is illegitimate the lockout is unlawful, and the NLRB can order it to reinstate workers with full back wages.[227] A lockout is also unlawful if the employer's intent is to destroy or eliminate the union.

The NLRB may rule that a bargaining position is illegitimate if the employer:

• Engages in bad-faith bargaining
• Insists on nonmandatory subjects of bargaining
• Makes unilateral changes
• Refuses to provide relevant information
• Hires permanent replacements
• Commits other ULPs that affect negotiations

Bad-faith bargaining. A lockout is unlawful if the employer refuses to bargain, reneges on agreements, maintains a take-it-or-leave-it attitude, or demands that the union abdicate its representational rights.[228]

Insistence on a permissive subject. A lockout to force the union to agree to a permissive bargaining subject is unlawful.[229] Permissive subjects include demands that the union:

• Withdraw a ULP charge, contract grievance, or lawsuit

- Change the scope of the bargaining unit
- Reimburse the employer for property damage
- Change ratification procedures

See additional examples on pages 117–118.

Unilateral change. A lockout is tainted if the employer implements a contract proposal or makes other changes before reaching a good faith impasse with the union.[230] For more discussion, see pages 26–27.

Failure to provide requested information. A lockout may be ruled unlawful if the employer fails to answer union requests for information relevant to the bargaining process.[231]

Hiring permanent replacements. An employer may continue operations during a lockout with supervisors, nonunit personnel, employees from other locations, and temporary replacements. But hiring permanent replacements makes a lockout unlawful.[232]

Partial lockout

An employer may retain workers during a lockout if it makes its selections for substantial business reasons and not on the basis of union membership. In one case, the Board allowed an employer to keep nonstrikers and crossovers while locking out everyone else.[233] In another, it permitted an employer to retain probationary employees.[234]

UI benefits

In 34 states and Puerto Rico, locked out workers can qualify for unemployment insurance (UI). (See list on page 92.) In other states and territories, benefits are denied under the labor dispute disqualification.

Eligibility. Each jurisdiction that provides benefits has its own eligibility criteria. For instance, Massachusetts pays unless the lockout is in reaction to substantial and repeated property damage. California and Utah pay unless the employer is a member of a multi-employer bargaining association that gives notice that if the union strikes one member, the others will lock out. Indiana does not pay if bargaining is at an impasse. Mississippi requires evidence that the lockout is unjustified. Wisconsin and New

Jersey do not pay if the lockout comes on the heels of a strike. Unions should review their state UI law.

BARGAINING THREAT

Q. Management says if we don't agree to its final offer, it will lock us out. Isn't this bad-faith bargaining?

A. No. An employer can threaten a lockout to pressure a union to accept its contract proposals.

WARN LAW

Q. Doesn't the federal WARN law require an employer to give 60 days notice before initiating a lockout?

A. No. The WARN law does not apply to a lawful lockout.[235]

SCAB PAY

Q. If our employer locks us out and hires new workers, can it pay the replacements more than the rates it is offering us in bargaining?

A. No, not unless it is unable to recruit workers at the bargaining-table rate.

PERMANENT SUBCONTRACT

Q. Can an employer permanently subcontract bargaining unit work during a lockout?

A. The authorities are in conflict. The Board says permanent subcontracting during a lockout is illegal.[236] The D.C. Court of Appeals disagrees.[237]

REVIVING AN UNLAWFUL LOCKOUT

Q. We filed charges that the company's lockout is illegal because one of its purposes is to make the union drop a lawsuit. If the employer withdraws this demand, will its lockout become lawful?

A. No. The only way to cure an unlawful lockout is to reinstate employees and reimburse them for lost wages.[238]

HEALTH INSURANCE

Q. Can an employer cancel health insurance during a lockout?

A. Yes.

SEARCH REQUIREMENTS

Q. If I file for UI benefits during a lockout, will I have to look for new work?

A. Yes.

SUPPORTIVE LOCKOUT

Q. Can an employer lock out its employees because the union is striking a competing firm?

A. Yes, if the companies have agreed among themselves that if one is struck the others will lock out.[239]

VACATION PAY

Q. Must an employer pay accrued vacation pay to locked out employees?

A. Yes.[240]

Glossary

Ally Business closely integrated with the struck employer or performing struck work.

Ambulatory picketing Picketing an employer whose worksite is mobile and changing.

Administrative Law Judge (ALJ) Presides over NLRB hearings and issues recommended decisions on unfair labor practices.

Board Five-person NLRB panel that reviews ALJ rulings.

Circuit courts System of 12 federal courts with power to affirm or vacate Board decisions.

Common situs Location on which two or more employers engage in normal business operations.

Contractors' gate Entrance reserved for contractors performing work that is unrelated to the employer's regular operations and which, if carried out while the plant was operating regularly, would not require a partial or total curtailment of operations.

Conversion Transformation of an economic strike to a ULP strike.

Economic strike Strike to obtain movement in collective bargaining.

FMCS Federal Mediation and Conciliation Service.

Impasse Stalemate in negotiations in which neither party is willing to make further concessions.

Off-duty picketing Picketing by employees still on the job.

Injunction Order by state or federal judge; often limits numbers and locations of union pickets.

Intermittent strike Repeated walkouts designed to confuse and unsettle an employer.

Lockout Temporary shutdown of plant or facility to gain advantage in collective bargaining or to avoid the consequences of a surprise strike.

Mandatory bargaining subject Matter directly relating to terms or conditions of employment.

NLRA National Labor Relations Act.

NLRB National Labor Relations Board.

Partial strike Refusal to perform assigned or expected duties.

Permissive bargaining subject Matter which involves internal union affairs, which indirectly affects employees, or which is within managerial prerogatives.

Primary employer Employer with whom the union has a labor dispute.

Reserved gate Entrance reserved for struck employer, its employees, agents, and suppliers.

Secondary picketing Picketing an employer with whom the union does not have a dispute to force that employer to cease doing business with the primary employer or to induce its employees to strike.

Secondary employer Employer other than the struck employer or its allies.

Secondary employee Employee of a secondary employer.

Section 8(b)(4) Section of NLRA that forbids secondary picketing and other coercive activity against secondary employers.

Slowdown Reduction of employee output or operations without a full-scale strike.

Sympathy strike Refusal of persons outside the bargaining unit to cross a union picket line.

Unfair labor practice (ULP) Violation of NLRA by employer or union.

Unfair-labor-practice strike (ULP strike) Strike caused, at least in part, by employer NLRA violations.

Unilateral change Change in mandatory subject of bargaining without prior notice to the union or adequate opportunity to bargain.

Endnotes

The endnotes cite NLRB and court decisions. The NLRB publishes decisions in a reporter called Decisions and Orders of the National Labor Relations Board, abbreviated as NLRB.

The citation International Paper Co., 319 NLRB 1253, 1266 (1995) refers to a decision in volume 319 of the NLRB reporter beginning on page 1253. Page 1266 of the decision discusses the particular matter referred to in the text or is the page where a quote originates.

NLRB decisions are available on the NLRB website: *www.nlrb.gov*. First click Decisions. Then click Board Decisions. Then click the volume number. Then click the name of the case. The website currently goes back to volume 258 (1981). Older decisions are being added.

Federal circuit court decisions are cited as follows: Culinary Workers Local 226 v. NLRB, 309 F.3d 578, 582 (9th Cir. 2002). The decision is found in volume 309 of a series called Federal Reporter Third Series, beginning on page 578. Circuit court decisions after 1995 can be located on the FindLaw website: *www.findlaw.com*. Click the appropriate circuit and type in the names of the parties.

U.S. Supreme court decisions are cited as: Golden State Transit Corp. v. Los Angeles, 493 U.S. 103 (1989). This case is in volume 493 of a reporter called U.S. Reports, beginning on page 103. It can be found on the FindLaw website.

1. Rail and air carriers are governed by the Railway Labor Act (RLA), a federal law that permits strikes but imposes excessive waiting periods. Federal employees are prohibited from striking. State and local government workers are regulated by state public-sector bargaining laws, 14 of which (Alaska, California, Hawaii, Idaho, Illinois, Louisiana, Minnesota, Montana, Ohio, Oregon, Pennsylvania, Vermont, Wisconsin, and Wyoming) permit strikes to some degree. Farm worker rights depend on state law.

2. *See* Boghosian Raisin Packing Co., Inc., 342 NLRB No. 32 (2004) (employees who took part in strike lost status as employees, allowing employer to refuse reinstatement: union sent 60-day termination notice but because of clerical error, failed to notify federal and state mediation agencies). **Note:** The Board acknowledged that had the strike been a ULP strike, the sanctions imposed by §8(d) could not have applied (slip opinion at p.4).

3. *See* Brotherhood of Locomotive Firemen and Enginemen v. NLRB, 302 F.2d 198 (9th Cir. 1962) (state labor agency which had no funds or staff for mediation and merely filed notices of labor dispute was not an agency to which union must provide notice under §8(d)(1)).

4. *See* Retail Clerks Assn. Local 219 v. NLRB, 265 F.2d 814, 819 (D.C. Cir. 1959) ("Thus if untimely notice were given [to the mediation agencies], the union would have committed a violation of Section 8(d)(3). If, however, the union were to wait for 30 days beyond the Section 8(d)(3) notice, and then go out on strike, it would not be in violation of Section 8(d)(4)."); Fort Smith Chair Co., 143 NLRB 514, 519 (1963) ("[W]here late notices under Section 8(d)(3) to the Mediation and Conciliation Service are filed, the waiting period must be extended to include a full 30 days after the filing of such notices in order to give mediation its intended statutory period in which to work.").

5. Bi-County Wholesale Beverage Distributors, 291 NLRB 466, 468-469 (1988).

6. 29 U.S.C. §158(d)(4)(B).

7. 29 U.S.C. §142(2).

8. Culinary Workers Local 226 v. NLRB, 309 F.3d 578, 582 (9th Cir. 2002) ("[A]n employer must maintain the *status quo* after the expiration of a collective-bargaining agreement until a new collective-bargaining agreement has been negotiated or the parties have bargained to impasse."). **Note:** When a contract expires, a union can file a unilateral-change charge to enforce a term of the agreement that had been followed by the parties, a past practice independent of the contract, or a past practice that conflicts with the contract. The Sacramento Union, 258 NLRB 1074, 1075 (1981). It cannot, however, enforce an interpretation of the expired contract that has not previously been followed. *See* NCR Corp., 271 NLRB 1212, 1213 (1984).

9. **Note:** The employer is not *compelled* to cancel the check-off procedure. *See* Frito-Lay, Inc., 243 NLRB 137, 139 (1979).

10. *See* Arizona Portland Cement Co., 281 NLRB 304 fn.2 (1986).

11. Bottom Line Enterprises, 302 NLRB 373, 374 (1991) ("[W]hen, as here, the parties are engaged in negotiations, an employer's obligation to refrain from unilateral changes extends beyond the mere duty to give notice and an opportunity to bargain; it encompasses a duty to refrain from implementation at all, unless and until an overall impasse has been reached on bargaining for the agreement as a whole."). **Note:** The Board recognizes limited exceptions to enable the employer to deal with economic emergencies or to resolve "discrete events" such as an annual adjustment to health care benefits. *See* Stone Container Corp., 313 NLRB 336, 336-337 (1993). **Further note:** The Fifth Circuit does not require an employer to bargain the entire contract to impasse before making a unilateral change in a deadlocked matter. Nabors Trailers, Inc. v. NLRB, 910 F.2d 268, 273 (5th Cir. 1990).

12. *See* The Hotel Roanoke, 293 NLRB 182, 184 (1989) ("The piecemeal introduction of ... significant new bargaining demands at comparatively late stages in negotiations could only have hampered the bargaining process and lessened the likelihood of the parties reaching an agreement and thus constitutes additional evidence of bad-faith bargaining."); Yearbook House, 223 NLRB 1456, 1465 (1976) (addition of 13 predictably unacceptable proposals, 11 months after bargaining began, bad-faith bargaining).

13. Available from *Labor Notes*, 7435 Michigan Avenue, Detroit, Michigan 48224 ($24.00).

14. *See* New York University Medical Center, 261 NLRB 822, 824 (1982).

15. *See* Gainesville Mfg. Co., 271 NLRB 1186, 1188 (1984) ("close presence of the representatives of the [employer] during the handbilling constituted [improper] surveillance of union activities....").

16. Poly-America, Inc., 328 NLRB 667, 668 (1999).

17. United Parcel Service, Inc., 331 NLRB 338, 338 (2000).

18. Superior Emerald Park Landfill, LLC, 340 NLRB No. 54 (2003).

19. *See* Miller Industries Towing Equipment, Inc., 342 NLRB No. 112 fn. 3. (2004).

20. National Steel & Shipbuilding Co., 324 NLRB 499, 499-502 (1997) (employer may not videotape pre-work rallies absent showing of reasonable, objective basis for anticipating misconduct).

21. Escanaba Paper Co., 314 NLRB 732, 734 (1994).

22. United Parcel Service, 195 NLRB 441, 448-450 (1972).

23. Pay 'N Save Corp., 247 NLRB 1346, 1346 (1980).

24. Wolfie's, 159 NLRB 686, 694-695 (1966) (rejecting employer's contention that to permit employees working on one shift to picket the next is to require the employer "to finance the pickets").

25. Thrift Drug Co., 204 NLRB 41, 42-43 (1973) (employer unlawfully suspended employee who, while picketing during her off hours, convinced driver delivering merchandise to turn around); Wolfies, 159 NLRB 686, 694-695 (1966).

26. E.L. Wiegand Div. v. NLRB, 650 F.2d 463, 474 (3d Cir. 1981) ("[A]n employee who pickets during off-duty time cannot be regarded as a 'striker' against whom an employer can act.").

27. Riverside Cement Co., 296 NLRB 840, 841 (1989).

28. Walkouts over pre-expiration grievances may be barred by the expired contract's no-strike clause. Goya Foods, Inc., 238 NLRB 1465, 1466-1467 (1978).

29. For cases finding two stoppages protected (but not in an inside campaign) *see* Chelsea Homes, Inc., 298 NLRB 813, 831 (1990) ("[T]wo stoppages, even of like nature, are insufficient to constitute evidence of a pattern of recurring, and therefore unprotected, stoppages."); Robertson Industries, 216 NLRB 361 (1975) (two one-day work stoppages in three months, protected); NLRB v. Empire Gas, Inc., 566 F.2d 681, 686 (10th Cir. 1977) (one-day stoppage followed by two-day stoppage, protected). Multiple walkouts are more likely to be granted legal protection if each protests a separate unfair labor practice. *See* Blades Mfg. Corp., 144 NLRB 561, 566 (1963) ("If the employees struck repeatedly, it was because the Respondent repeatedly denied them their statutory rights.").

30. *See* United States Service Industries, Inc., 315 NLRB 285, 285 (1994).

31. Ramada Inn, 201 NLRB 431, 436-437 (1973) (four hours after start of strike, union sent telegram unconditionally offering to return to work the following day; replacement of one employee after receipt of telegram violated §8(a)(3)).

32. Huck Manufacturing Co., 254 NLRB 739, 747-749 (1981).

33. Chrysler Corp., 228 NLRB 486, 490 (1977).

34. *See* Coast Engraving, Inc., 282 NLRB 1236 fn. 1 and 1251-1252 (1987). **Note:** Workers who repeatedly refuse overtime requests to advance an inside campaign, even when this is protected, can be classified as strikers—allowing the employer to hire permanent replacements who will perform the duties. *See* Prince Lithograph Co., Inc., 205 NLRB 110 fn.2 (1973).

35. *See* Highland Superstores, Inc., 314 NLRB 146 (1994).

36. Savage Gateway Supermarket, Inc., 286 NLRB 180, 183-84 (1987).

37. *See* Safety Kleen Oil Services, Inc., 308 NLRB 208, 209 (1992) ("The Board has found a sickout to be protected concerted activity in those cases where there is evidence that the employer knew or had reason to know that the employees were not really sick, but were engaged in a work stoppage to protest their working conditions.").

38. *See* Garland Coal & Mining Co. v. UMWA District 21, 778 F.2d 1297, 1303 (8th Cir. 1985).

39. *See* Shelly & Anderson Furn. Mfg. Co., 199 NLRB 250, 263-65 (1972).

40. Harvey Manufacturing, Inc., 309 NLRB 465, 468-471 (1992) (suggesting that Board might rule differently if employer could show that the five-day agreement was necessary to persuade the contractor to supply replacements).

41. The Clarion Hotel-Marin, 279 NLRB 481, 492 (1986).

42. Hospital Episcopal San Lucas, 319 NLRB 54, 59 (1995) (violation basis of ULP strike).

43. *See* NLRB. v. Federal Security, Inc., 154 F.3d 751, 755-757 (7th Cir. 1998) (employer can discharge workers who leave posts without taking necessary precautions). **Note:** The mere danger of economic loss, such as the possibility of product spoilage, is not the sort of injury that forces the union to give prior notice. Leprino Cheese Mfg. Co., 170 NLRB 601, 606-607 (1968).

44. 29 U.S.C. §158(g).

45. Earlier Board decisions allowing health care unions a 72-hour window to strike
    after the notice date and time were overruled in 2003. Alexandria Clinic, P.A.,
    339 NLRB 1262 (2003).

46. *See, e.g.*, Howard Gault Co. v. Texas Rural Legal Aid, Inc., 848 F.2d 544, 561
    (5th Cir. 1988) (statute forbidding picketing by more than two persons within
    50 feet of an entrance, unconstitutional); United Food & Commercial Workers
    v. IBP, Inc., 857 F.2d 422 , 430-432 (8th Cir. 1988) (statute requiring pickets to
    stand at least 50 feet from each other, unconstitutional); Edwards v. City of
    Coeur d'Alene, 262 F.3d 856, 863-867 (9th Cir. 2001) (city ordinance banning
    wooden or plastic supports for picket signs, unconstitutional); Local 391,
    International Brotherhood of Teamsters v. City of Rocky Mount, 672 F.2d 376
    (4th Cir. 1982) (city ordinance requiring prior permit for picketing, unconsti-
    tutional).

47. Gainesville Mfg. Co., 271 NLRB 1186, 1187–1188 (1984) (driveway entrance);
    Venetian Casino Resort, LLC., 345 NLRB No. 82 (2005) (private sidewalk con-
    necting two public sidewalks along roadway).

48. Republic Aviation Corp. v. NLRB., 324 U.S. 793 (1945); Town & Country
    Supermarkets, 340 NLRB No. 172 (2004).

49. Jean Country, 291 NLRB 11, 13 (1988) (taking into account "the safety of
    attempting communications at alternative public sites"). *See* W.S. Butterfield,
    Inc., 292 NLRB 30, 30-34 (1988) (picketing on public street ineffective and
    unsafe); Medina Super Duper, 286 NLRB 728, 730 (1987) ("[W]e find that the
    §7 right exercised by the Union outweighs the Respondent's property right to
    exclude striking employees from picketing and handbilling in front of its store.").
    Note: If the employer leases its facilities from a third party, the employer may
    not have a sufficient property interest to exclude pickets. *See* Wild Oats Com-
    munity Markets, 336 NLRB 179, 180-182 (2001).

50. *See* Ornamental Iron Work Co., 295 NLRB 473, 479 (1989) (in view of "the
    traditional right of pickets to take steps necessary to perfect a verbal appeal to a
    driver headed for a strike-bound facility … an instantaneous blockage, which
    allows those seeking access to freely choose between disregarding or honoring
    the picket line, fails to convert protected into unprotected strike action.").

51. *See* Golden State Transit Corp. v. Los Angeles, 493 U.S.103 (1989). *See also*
    American Postal Workers Union, Local 96 v. Memphis, 361 F.3d 898 (6th Cir.
    2004) (union allowed to sue city, employer, and security guard agency for con-
    spiracy when on-duty police officers and off-duty officers on private details
    undertook policy of arresting strikers without cause while failing to prevent
    supervisors from driving into picket lines).

52. *See, e.g.*, Scott Hudgens II, 230 NLRB 414 (1977) (shopping center); Holland
    Rantos Co., Inc., 234 NLRB 726 (1978) (industrial park).

53. Little & Co., 296 NLRB 691, 692-693 (1989).

54. Letter Carriers v. Austin, 418 U.S. 264, 283 (1974) ("[F]ederal law gives a union
    license to use intemperate, abusive, or insulting language without fear of restraint
    or penalty if it believes such rhetoric to be an effective means to make its point.");
    Professional Porter & Window Cleaning Co., 263 NLRB 136, 139 fn. 12 (1982)
    ("[T]he truth or falsity of a communication is not material and is not the test of
    its protected character."); United Parcel Service, Inc., 234 NLRB 223, 227-228
    (1978) (union newsletter alleging that employer buys arbitrators and judges, pro-
    tected by NLRA); Yeger v. Teamsters Local 20, 114 LRRM 3583, (Ohio Ct.

App. 1982) (signs calling general manager a nazi, and accusing him of using gestapo tactics and maintaining a concentration camp atmosphere, not subject to defamation suit).

55. *See* Steam Press Holdings, Inc. v. Hawaii Teamsters Local 996, 302 F.3d 998, 1006 (9th Cir. 2002) (in labor dispute "even seemingly 'factual' statements take on an appearance more closely resembling opinion than objective fact").

56. *See* NMC Finishing v. NLRB, 101 F.3d 528 (8th Cir. 1996) (sign: "Who is Rhonda f/sucking today?").

57. *See* The Sacramento Union, 291 NLRB 540 fn.1 (1988) (letters to newspaper's advertisers asserting that newspaper is "speeding downhill," protected); Emarco, Inc., 284 NLRB 832 (1987) (telling contractor that employer does not pay its bills, and will not finish the job, protected).

58. Montefiore Hospital v. NLRB, 621 F.2d 510, 517 (2nd Cir. 1980) (doctor's discharge sustained for telling patients they would not be taken care of at struck hospital); Coca Cola Bottling Works, Inc., 186 NLRB 1050, 1054 (1970) (assertions that mice droppings were present in struck soda bottles).

59. Detroit Newspaper Agency, 342 NLRB No. 24, slip op. at 120–124 (2004).

60. 29 U.S.C. §158(b)(4).

61. Local 761, International Union of Electrical Workers v. NLRB, 366 U.S. 667, 673 (1961).

62. OCAW Local 4-449 (Anchortank), 238 NLRB 290 (1978), *enforced*, 601 F.2d 233, 240 (5th Cir. 1979) ("A striking union may supplement its picketing of the premises with non-situs requests to honor the picket line directed to the same employees who ordinarily would encounter the pickets."); *cf.* Teamsters Local 200 (Milwaukee Plywood), 126 NLRB 650, 650 (1960) (union did not violate Section 8(b)(4)(A) by instructing members to observe picket line at customer facility"). *But cf.* Teamsters Local 688 (Frito-Lay), 345 NLRB No. 96 (2005) (Teamsters union violated no-strike clause by ordering members to exercise contractual right to honor third-party picket line).

63. UFCW Local 1996 (Visiting Nurse Health System), 336 NLRB 421 (2001).

64. *See* Oil Workers (Firestone Tire & Rubber), 173 NLRB 1244, 1245 (1968) (repair of water treatment system).

65. The rule allowing related-work picketing of reserve gates does not apply at construction sites. Building & Const. Trades Council (Markwell & Hartz, Inc.), 155 NLRB 319 (1967).

66. *See* Central Soya Co., Inc., 288 NLRB 1402, 1406 (1988).

67. But pickets can ask secondary employees not to provide services or give other assistance to the struck employer. IBEW Local 3 (New Power Wire & Electric), 144 NLRB 1089, 1094-1095 (1963).

68. *See* IBEW Local 3 (New Power Wire & Electric), 144 NLRB 1089, 1092-1095 (1963) (union not required to forego further picketing where it was successful in reducing the employer's work force so that the employer had to suspend work temporarily); IBEW Local 861 (Brownfield Electric), 145 NLRB 1163, 1165-1166 (1964).

69. IBEW Local 970 (Interox America), 306 NLRB 54, 59-60 (1992) (out-of-way gate lawful unless employer deliberately chooses location to inhibit the union's ability to communicate).

70. The manager must notify the picketing union that the gates have been reestablished and will be properly maintained in the future. Carpenters Local 470 (Muller-Anderson), 224 NLRB 315, 316 (1976).

71. NLRB Casehandling Manual §10266.2. See text at note 201 *infra*.

72. 29 U.S.C. §§106-108. **Note:** Board-requested injunctions are exempt from these requirements.

73. States and territories with "baby" Norris LaGuardia Acts include California, Connecticut, Hawaii, Idaho, Indiana, Louisiana, Maine, Maryland, Massachusetts, Minnesota, New Jersey, New York, North Dakota, Oregon, Pennsylvania, Puerto Rico, Rhode Island, Utah, Washington, and Wisconsin.

74. 29 U.S.C §§178-180.

75. *See* NLRB v. Florida Dept. of Bus. Reg., 868 F.2d 391, 394-396 (11th Cir. 1989).

76. Lundy Packing Co., 223 NLRB 139, 157 (1976) ("[T]here was nothing improper in an arrangement whereby additional employees would be called upon to join the strike as the strike progressed.").

77. NationsRent, Inc., 342 NLRB No. 19 (2004). *But see* The Greenbrier, 340 NLRB No. 92 (2003) (employer engaged in illegal interference when it contacted police to ask them to remove pickets because they lacked a permit which the city attorney had said was not necessary).

78. Genesco, Inc. v. Joint Council 13, United Shoe Workers, 230 F.Supp. 923, 931 (S.D.N.Y. 1964).

79. National Steel & Shipbuilding Co., 324 NLRB 499, 535 (1977) ("[I]t may be presumed that the mere presence of the camera will inhibit or chill [employees] in saying or doing things that are nevertheless protected by Section 7."). *See also* Kentucky River Medical Center, 340 NLRB No. 71, sl. op. at 33 (2003) (pointing camera at pickets without pressing "on" button, illegal).

80. *See* Williamhouse-Regency of Delaware, 297 NLRB 199, 199 (1989), *enforced*, 915 F.2d 631, 635 (11th Cir. 1990) ("In the collective bargaining setting [a] contract offer is not automatically terminated by the other party's rejection or counterproposal, but may be accepted within a reasonable time unless it was expressly withdrawn prior to acceptance, was expressly made contingent upon some condition subsequent, or was made subject to intervening circumstances which made it unfair to hold the offeror to his bargain.").

81. *See* Romal Iron Works Corp., 285 NLRB 1178, 1182 (1989) ("niggers," "Polacks," "spics"); Domsey Trading Corp., 310 NLRB 777, 793 (1993) ("whores," "monkeys").

82. *See* Facet Enterprises, Inc., 290 NLRB 152, 153 (1988).

83. Heritage Container, Inc., 334 NLRB 455, 460 (2001).

84. 29 U.S.C. §504(a).

85. 29 U.S.C. §2102(b)(2)(A). *See* Teamsters Nat'l Freight Indus. Negotiating Comm. v. Churchill Truck Lines, Inc., 935 F.Supp. 1021, 1026 (W.D. Mo.1996).

86. *See* L.A. Water Treatment, Division of Chromalloy American Corp., 286 NLRB 868, 872 (1987). **Note:** By changing a few words, the employer could have issued a lawful permanent replacement letter.

87. 20 C.F.R. §652.9(a).

88. *See* Briggs Transp. Co. v. International Bhd. of Teamsters, 739 F.2d 341 (8th Cir. 1984).

89. NLRB v. Fruit and Vegetable Packers, Local 760 (Tree Fruits Labor Relations Committee, Inc.), 377 U.S. 58 (1964). **Note:** A struck product is the product of the employer with whom the union has a labor dispute. A producer of a product "encompasses anyone who enhances the economic value of the product ultimately sold or consumed" with no distinction drawn between processors, distributors, and those supplying services. Great Western Broadcast Corp., 150 NLRB 467, 472 (1964).

90. NLRB. v. Retail Store Emp. Union, Local 1001, 447 U.S. 607, 614-615 (1980).

91. Lechmere, Inc. v. NLRB, 502 U.S. 527 (1992).

92. *See* Great American, 322 NLRB 17, 23-24 (1996) (supermarket that allowed musical societies doing Christmas gift wrapping and Salvation Army to solicit on premises may not bar union handbilling). **Note:** The second, fourth, and sixth circuits require a showing that the retailer has permitted solicitation by other labor or employer organizations. *See, e.g.,* Cleveland Real Estate Partners v. NLRB, 95 F.3d 457 (6th Cir. 1996).

93. *See* Southern Council of Industrial Workers (Missoula White Pine Sash Co.), 301 NLRB 410 fn.3 (1991) ("Huttig's control over labor relations of Southern and Missoula is sufficient to deny Missoula the protection of Sec. 8(b)(4)(B).").

94. Los Angeles Newspaper Guild Local 69 (Hearst Corp.), 185 NLRB 303 (1970). *See also* UFCW Local 1059 (Days Inn), 268 NLRB 595 (1984) (two motels owned by same corporation, not allies).

95. **Note:** Even if employees at allied enterprises continue to work, a picket line may achieve its goal by interfering with deliveries. *See* Teamsters Local 179 (Alexander Warehouse), 128 NLRB 916 (1960).

96. National Maritime Union Local 333 (D. M. Picton & Co.), 131 NLRB 693, 699 (1961). **Note:** The D.C. Circuit disagrees that the struck employer must make the arrangement and would allow a union to picket a company which takes over the work of a struck employer at the request of a customer. Laborers Local 859 v. NLRB, 446 F.2d 1319, 1321 (D.C. Cir. 1971).

97. *See* Central Illinois Public Service Co., 326 NLRB 928, 935, 995 (1998) ("A bargaining representative is entitled to information as to whether and to what extent during a strike or lockout, the employer is using outside firms to perform unit work.").

98. International Longshoremen's Ass'n (Coastal Stevedoring), 313 NLRB 412, 415-417 (1993).

99. International Longshoremen's Ass'n. v. NLRB, 56 F.3d 205, 213 (D.C. Cir. 1995).

100. Teamsters Local 324 (Truck Operators League of Oregon), 122 NLRB 25, 27 (1958) (picketing lawful because the union picketed employers "to the extent that they were acting as allies." *See* California Motor Express, NLRB Div. of Advice, 1974 WL 37657, June 23, 1974.

101. Service Employees Local 254 (United Bldg. Maint. Corp.), 173 NLRB 280, 285-286 (1968).

102. Prater v. United Mine Workers of America, Districts 20 and 23, 793 F.2d 1201, 1206-1207 (11th Cir. 1986).

103. Coercive activity against employer collective-bargaining representatives violates §8(b)(1)(B) of the NLRA. But residential picketing, in the absence of excessive noise or threats, is not coercive. *See* Carpenters Local 1098 (Milton J. Womack), 280 NLRB 875 fn.1 (1986) (peaceful picketing of home of employer's vice president and chief negotiator, not unlawful).

104. Frisby v. Schultz, 487 U.S. 474, 483 (1988).

105. Arapahoe County, Colorado, Ordinance 2000-1 (defining block as 660 feet).

106. *See* Kirkeby v. Furness, 92 F.3d 655, 661 (8th Cir. 1996) (200-foot buffer zone).

107. *See* State v. Castellano, 506 N.W.2d 641, 647 (Minn. App. 1993).

108. Hebrew Home & Hospital for Chronic Sick, Inc. v. Davis, 235 N.Y.S. 2d 318, 324 (N.Y. Sup. Ct. 1962). *But see* Annenberg v. Southern Cal. Dist. Council of Laborers, 38 Cal. App. 3d 637 (Cal. App. 4 Dist. 1974) (picketing outside private estate surrounded by golf course, security guards, and protective fence did not invade homeowner's right to privacy).

109. Codified as 29 U.S.C. §158(b)(1)(A).

110. *See* CWA Local 1118 (New York Telephone), 305 NLRB 770 fn.1 (1991).

111. The hotel does not qualify as an ambulatory situs because the president is not performing his normal business there.

112. SEIU Local 525 (Lerner Enterprises), 329 NLRB 638 fn. 12 (1999).

113. Teamsters Local 612 (AAA Motor Lines), 211 NLRB 608, 610-611 (1974).

114. Teamsters Local 200 (Reilly Cartage), 183 NLRB 305, 305 (1970).

115. Teamsters Local 688 (Acme Paper Co.), 121 NLRB 702, 703-704 (1958).

116. Teamsters Local 83 (Allied Concrete), 231 NLRB 1097, 1098 (1977) .

117. IBEW Local 861 (Plauche Electric), 135 NLRB 250, 255 (1962) ("Manifestly, Plauche's normal business at the common situs did not come to an end merely because his employees temporarily departed under these circumstances.").

118. Teamsters Local 379 (Catalano Bros.), 175 NLRB 459, 461 (1969) (asking secondary's employees not to unload truck "amounted to no more than lawful requests to honor a primary picket line"); Teamsters Local 542 (Shaker Express), 191 NLRB 515, 525 (1971) (union representative can inform customer's employees that they have right to refuse to accept delivery of primary's freight).

119. Edward J. DeBartolo Corp. v. Florida Gulf Coast Bldg. & Const. Trades Council, 485 U.S. 568, 583-588 (1988). **Note:** The notion that the Taft-Hartley Act forbids secondary boycotts is inaccurate. The term "secondary boycott" does not appear in the act. What Taft-Hartley forbids is coercion of a secondary or inducement of its employees.

120. Hospital and Service Employees Union, Local 399 (Delta Air Lines), 293 NLRB 602 (1989).

121. The Board has not ruled on bannering, but several ALJs have found that in the absence of confrontational conduct or signals the practice neither coerces the secondary employer nor induces its employees. *See e.g.,* Carpenters Local 184 and 1498 (Grayhawk Development), NLRB Div. of Judges, 2005 WL 195115, January 13, 2005. The federal court for the 9th Circuit has issued a strong decision finding bannering lawful. Overstreet v. Carpenters Local Union No. 1506, 409 F.3d 1199 (9th Cir. 2005) (banner identifying secondary as being involved in "labor dispute" not Taft-Hartley violation).

122. Laborers Local 79 (C&D Restoration, Inc.), NLRB Div. of Advice, 2003 WL 23469281 fn.8, August 15, 2003.

123. Chicago Typographical Union No. 16 (Alden Press), 151 NLRB 1666, 1668-1669 (1965).

124. *See* Great American, 322 NLRB 17, 23-24 (1996).

125. Storer Communications, Inc. v. National Ass'n of Broadcast Employees & Technicians, 854 F.2d 144, 147 (6th Cir. 1988) ("Since the handbilling itself was not proscribed activity, peaceful warnings that handbilling will occur are not unlawful.").

126. Carpenters Local 745 (Sheraton Corp.), NLRB Div. of Advice, 1991 WL 25321, January 23, 1991.

127. Petrochem Insulation, Inc., 330 NLRB 47, 49-50 (1999) (leaving open whether a meritless or sham filing against a secondary would also be immune from §8(b)(4) prosecution).

128. *See* Delta-Sonic Carwash Systems, Inc. v. Building Trades Council, AFL-CIO, 640 N.Y.S.2d 368, 372-376 (N.Y. Sup. 1995).

129. 29 U.S.C. §157.

130. P. B. & S. Chemical Co. Inc, 321 NLRB 525, 525 (1996) ("[T]he motive of employees who refuse to cross a lawful picket line is irrelevant to whether the refusal is protected under the Act."). **Note:** The fourth and sixth circuits take a more limited view. NLRB v. Union Carbide Corp., 440 F.2d 54, 56 (4th Cir. 1971) (refusal based on fear of violence, unprotected); Kellogg Co. v. NLRB, 457 F.2d 519, 523 (6th Cir. 1972). **Further note:** Nonunion workers who refuse to cross picket lines at a "stranger employer" have a weaker legal status than respecting a line at their own workplace. *See* NLRB v. William S. Carroll, Inc., 578 F.2d 1 (1st Cir. 1978).

131. *See* Buckley v. Bethlehem Steel Corp., 293 N.E.2d 248 (N.Y. 1972).

132. Pilot Freight Carriers, Inc., 224 NLRB 341, 341-342 (1976). Serious unfair labor practices for this purpose are those that are "destructive to the foundations on which collective bargaining must rest." Arlan's Dep't Store, 133 NLRB 802, 808 (1961).

133. Codified as 29 U.S.C. §143.

134. Plain Dealer Pub. Co. v. Cleveland Typographical Union, 520 F.2d 1220, 1228-1229 (6th Cir. 1975) ("[T]he evidence of threats and confrontations meets [the Section 502] standard"). *See also* West Penn Power Co., 89 LA 1227, 1231 (Hogler 1987) ("It is a recognized arbitral principle that employees who refuse to perform unsafe work are neither guilty of insubordination nor deemed to be strikers.").

135. American Transportation Service, Inc., 310 NLRB 294, 297 (1993).

136. *See* In re Teamsters Local 890, 225 B.R. 719 (Bkrtcy N.D. CA 1998).

137. *See* Trading Port, Inc., 219 NLRB 298, 299 fn.3 (1975) ("Strikers, whether economic or unfair-labor-practice strikers, are not entitled to compensation for the period they are on strike. Hence, Respondent was within its rights in

ceasing to pay its share of the premiums...the nonpayment of benefits to strikers during their period of striking is not a matter about which a company has an obligation to bargain....").

138. COBRA is short for the Consolidated Omnibus Budget Reconciliation Act of 1985. Part of the larger ERISA Act, its provisions apply to employers with 20 or more employees. Some states have similar laws for smaller employers.

139. 26 CFR §54.4980B-6 A-3(b) ("[T]he plan must inform the provider that the qualified beneficiary currently does not have coverage but will have coverage retroactively to the date coverage was lost if COBRA continuation coverage is elected.").

140. Reed National Corp. v. Director of DES, 473 N.E.2d 190, 192 (Mass.1985).

141. Oklahoma, Pennsylvania, Texas, and Wyoming, nominally work-stoppage states, consider a stoppage as a claimant's refusal to work, rather than a full or partial cessation of operations.

142. Hertz Corp. v. Acting Director of Div. of Emp. and Training, 771 N.E.2d 153, 157 (Mass. 2002) (no work stoppage although certain functions went unperformed while managers and nonstriking workers filled in for striking employees).

143. *See* Plumrose USA v. Review Bd., 654 N.E.2d 827 (Ind. 1995).

144. *See* Hoffman v. Unemp. Comp. Bd. of Rev., 574 A.2d 57, 62-64 (Pa. 1990).

145. *See* John Morrell & Co. v. South Dakota Dept. of Labor, Unemployment Ins. Div., 460 N.W.2d 141, 143-145 (S.D. 1990); In re Sarvis, 251 S.E.2d 434 (N.C. 1979).

146. Sunstar Foods, Inc., v. Uhlendorf, 310 N.W.2d 80, 85 (Minn. 1981).

147. *See, e.g.*, Union Spring & Mfg. Co. v. Unemp. Comp. Bd. of Rev., 436 A.2d 1048, 1051 (Pa. 1981); Bays v. Shenango Co., 559 N.E.2d 740 (Oh. 1990).

148. *See* Texaco, Inc., 285 NLRB 241, 246 (1987) (employer can challenge payment of benefits "by demonstrating reliance on a nondiscriminatory contract interpretation that is reasonable and ... arguably correct").

149. *See* Pressmen's Local No. 7 v. Chicago Tribune, 657 F.Supp 353, 355 (N.D. Ill. 1987) (union may arbitrate post-expiration vacation pay claims under "accrued benefit" theory).

150. Gulf & Western Mfg. Co., 286 NLRB 1122, 1123-1125 (1987) (employer may not discontinue health insurance premiums for employees receiving workers' compensation or sick leave during strike).

151. Conoco, Inc., 265 NLRB 819, 821-822 (1982).

152. Advertiser's Manufacturing Co., 294 NLRB 740, 743 (1989).

153. Burlington Homes, Inc., 246 NLRB 1029, 1030 (1979) ("Respondent's conduct in offering a higher starting wage to striker replacements had a potentially devastating impact upon the right of employees to strike ... We therefore conclude that Respondent's conduct was inherently destructive of employee rights protected by Section 7 and Section 13 of the Act and hence also violated Section 8(a)(3) of the Act."); Beverly Health and Rehabilitation Services, Inc., 335 NLRB 635, 638 (2001) ("[T]he unexplained and publicized offer of higher

wages to strike replacements can only be seen as designed further to undermine the Local Union in the eyes of the employees it represented. Accordingly, we adopt the judge's finding that that action violated Section 8(a)(1).").

154. C–Line Express, 292 NLRB 638, 639 (1989) (replacement information is "clearly relevant to the union in exercising its responsibilities as the exclusive representative of unit employees.").

155. *See* Page Litho, Inc., 311 NLRB 881, 882 (1993) (names, classifications, and payroll information). *See also* Diamond Walnut Growers, Inc., 312 NLRB 61, 67 (1993) (no clear and present danger where identity of those who threatened nonstrikers is unknown and no evidence of involvement by union officials or agents).

156. *See* River City Mechanical, 289 NLRB 1503, 1505 (1988).

157. Gloversville Embossing Corp., 297 NLRB 182, 187-190 (1989) (wage increase of $.25 an hour).

158. S&W Motor Lines, Inc., 236 NLRB 938, 951–952 (1978) ($50 per trip to non-striking over-the-road drivers, unlawful). Bonuses may be paid to supervisors or employees outside of the bargaining unit who fill in for strikers. World Publishing Co., 220 NLRB 1065, 1072 (1975).

159. NLRB v. Erie Resistor Corp., 373 U.S. 221, 231-237 (1963) (granting replacements 20 years of additional seniority, illegal). **Note:** To settle a strike, a union can agree to superseniority for strike replacements and crossovers. Gem City Ready Mix Co., 270 NLRB 1260, 1260-1261 (1984).

160. General Electric Co., 80 NLRB 510, 511-513 (1948).

161. *See, e.g.*, IBEW Local 165 v. Bradley, 499 N.E. 2d 577, 587-588 (Ill. App.1986) (gross wages plus $25). A fine based on take-home pay is more likely to be approved. **Note:** A minority of courts refuse enforcement if the union constitution does not specify that fines can be collected in court or does not specify the amount of fine for the particular infraction. *See* CWA Local 10517 v. Gann, 510 So.2d 781, 782-785 (Miss. 1987).

162. Pattern Makers' League of North America v. NLRB, 473 U.S. 95 (1985).

163. Sheet Metal Workers Local 9 (Concord Metal), 297 NLRB 86, 88-90 (1989).

164. UAW Local 449 (National Metalcrafters) v. NLRB, 865 F.2d 791, 797 (6th Cir. 1989).

165. *Compare* Kapiolani Med. Center for Women and Children v. Hawaii, 82 F.Supp. 2d 1151, 1158-1159 (D. Haw. 2000) (state law valid) *with* Illinois v. Federal Tool and Plastics, Division of V.C.A., 344 N.E.2d 1, 4-5 (Ill. 1975) (state law invalid).

166. *See* Wahl Clipper Corp., 195 NLRB 634, 636 (1972).

167. *See* NLRB v. Neuro Affiliates Co., 702 F.2d 184, 186-188 (9th Cir. 1983).

168. Pattern and Model Makers Ass'n (Michigan Model Mfg's Ass'n.), 310 NLRB 929, 930 (1993).

169. 18 U.S.C. §1231.

170. Sunland Constr. Co., Inc., 309 NLRB 1224, 1230-1231 (1992).

171. Consumers Power Co., 282 NLRB 130, 132 (1986) ("[W]hen an employee is discharged for conduct that is part of the *res gestae* of protected concerted activities, the relevant question is whether the conduct is so egregious as to take it outside the protection of the Act, or of such a character as to render the employee unfit for further service.").

172. Clear Pine Mouldings, Inc., 268 NLRB 1044, 1045-1047 (1984). **Note:** The term "nonstriker" encompasses supervisors, security guards, and independent contractors, as well as replacements and fellow employees.

173. Massachusetts Coastal Seafoods, Inc., 293 NLRB 496 fn.1 (1989).

174. *See* Leasco, Inc., 289 NLRB 549 fn.1 (1988) (verbal attacks must be of such a nature that they would cause a reasonable person to fear an "imminent physical confrontation").

175. Catalytic, Inc., 275 NLRB 97, 98 (1985).

176. *See* General Chemical Corp., 290 NLRB 76, 83 (1988); Calliope Designs, Inc., 297 NLRB 510, 521-22 (1989).

177. Ornamental Iron Work Co., 295 NLRB 473, 478–480 (1989).

178. Tube Craft. Inc., 287 NLRB 491, 492-493 (1987) (blocking incidents lasting 65, 50, 15 and 2½ minutes, egregious misconduct).

179. *See* Detroit Newspaper Agency, 342 NLRB No. 24, slip op. at p.120-125 (2004) (trespass arrests).

180. *See* M.P.C. Plating, Inc. v. NLRB, 953 F.2d 1018, 1023 (6th Cir. 1992).

181. Aztec Bus Lines, Inc., 289 NLRB 1021, 1027-1029 (1988); Champ Corp., 291 NLRB 803, 806-807 (1988).

182. Abilities and Goodwill, Inc., 241 NLRB 27 (1979).

183. KSM Industries, Inc., 336 NLRB 133, 145 (2001).

184 New Jersey Bell Tel. Co., 300 NLRB 42, 43 (1990). Certainteed Corp., 282 NLRB 1101, 1125 (1987); Pennsylvania Power & Light Co., 301 NLRB 1104, 1107-1108 (1991).

185. *See* Pepsi-Cola Bottling Co. of Fayetteville, Inc., 315 NLRB 882, 882 (1994).

186. Airport Aviation Services, 292 NLRB 823, 830 (1989).

187. *See* Detroit Newspaper Agency, 342 NLRB No. 24 (2004).

188. Hormigonera Del Toa, Inc., 311 NLRB 956, 957–958 and fn. 3 (1993).

189. *See* Metlox Mfg. Co., 153 NLRB 1388, 1396 (1965).

190. **Note:** The duty to reinstate does not apply to strikers who have resigned, taken equivalent employment elsewhere, or committed serious misconduct.

191. *See* Burns Motor Freight, Inc., 250 NLRB 276, 277-278 (1980) ("[T]iming is significant but not conclusive in establishing the basis for a strike.").

192. *See* Patrick & Co., 248 NLRB 390, 392-393 (1980).

193. *See* Pillowtex Corp., 241 NLRB 40, 47-48 (1979).

194. *See* Modern Mfg. Co., Inc., 292 NLRB 10 (1988).

195. *See* Langston Co.'s, Inc., 304 NLRB 1022, 1070 (1991).

196. Minnesota Mining and Manufacturing Co., 261 NLRB 27 (1982).

197. NLRB v. Truitt Mfg. Co., 351 U.S. 149, 152-154 (1956). *But see* The Nielsen Lithographing Co., 305 NLRB 697, 699-701 (1991) (claim of need for concessions in order to "compete" does not trigger duty to furnish financial information).

198. *See* Pirelli Cable Corp., 323 NLRB 1009, 1017 (1997) where the following question and answer mailed to employees was ruled unlawful because of its final sentence:

Q. If I go out on strike, can I lose my job?
A. Yes. The Company can continue operating the plant, and can hire strike replacements. If you strike in an attempt to force the Company to agree to the Union's economic demands or to force the Company to withdraw its economic demands, the Company may permanently replace you. When the strike ends you would not have a job if you had been permanently replaced.

199. Hospital Episcopal San Lucas, 319 NLRB 54, 58-59 (1995).

200. Vulcan-Hart Corp., 262 NLRB 167, 168 (1982).

201. "In cases involving an unfair labor practice accompanied by a strike allegedly in protest thereof, the Regional Office should determine the nature of the strike. If the evidence supports a finding of an unfair labor practice strike, the Regional Office should allege such status in the complaint and seek an open-ended order requiring the reinstatement, on application, of all qualified striking employees." NLRB Casehandling Manual §10266.2.

202. Outdoor Venture Corp., 327 NLRB 706, 709 (1999) ("In order to find that the strike had reconverted to an economic strike at the time of the offer to return, the unfair labor practices allegedly prolonging the strike (i.e., the settled allegations) must have been fully remedied.").

203. *See* Outdoor Ventures Corp., 327 NLRB 706, 709 (1999) ("Inasmuch as the 60-day posting period was still in effect at the time of the employees' unconditional offer to return, we cannot find that the unfair labor practices allegedly prolonging the strike were fully remedied or that the strike was converted into an economic strike at that time.").

204. Nassau Ins. Co., 280 NLRB 878 fn.3 and 891-892 (1986) ([T]he Union unlawfully insisted upon nonmandatory subjects of bargaining and engaged in a strike to support its demands for nonmandatory bargaining subjects. Such a strike is not only unprotected, but also is unlawful as a breach of the duty to bargain."). *See also* United Mine Workers (Pittston Coal Co.), NLRB Div. of Advice, 1989 WL 241696, June 23, 1989. **Note:** An employer may be able to declare a strike illegal and refuse to reinstate participants even if it has not previously contended that the union's strike demands are permissive or unlawful. *See* Pratt Towers, Inc., 338 NLRB No. 8, slip op. at 5 (2002).

205. Consolidation Coal Co., 266 NLRB 670, 672 (1983) (letter); Storer Communications, Inc., 294 NLRB 1056, 1093 (1989) (announcement).

206. *See* Hickinbotham Bros. Ltd., 254 NLRB 96, 102-103 (1981) ("A strike is a two-edged sword. Depending upon how it affects the employer's operations, the strikers may gain concessions or they may lose concessions previously obtained."). *Cf.* Storer Communications, 294 NLRB 1056 (1989) (withdrawal of proposals during ULP strike, unlawful).

207. *See* Steelworkers Local 8560 (Sparta Mfg. Co.), NLRB Div. of Advice, 103 LRRM 1238 (1979).

208. *See* Jacobs v. Georgia-Pacific Corp., 323 S.E.2d 238, 239 (Ga. App. 1984).

209. *See* Clow Water Systems Co., 317 NLRB 126, 128 (1995).

210. Eads Transfer, Inc., 304 NLRB 711, 712 (1991).

211. If the strike is a ULP strike, the employer is allowed a five-day grace period.

212. As explained in Chapter 2, the employer can disregard the expired agreement's dues-checkoff, union-security, and arbitration requirements.

213. Target Rock Corp., 324 NLRB 373, 374 (1997).
214. Rose Printing Co., 304 NLRB 1076, 1079 (1991). **Note:** *Rose* appears to conflict with the Supreme Court's assertion that "If and when a job for which the striker is qualified becomes available, he is entitled to an offer of reinstatement." NLRB v. Fleetwood Trailer Co., 389 U.S. 375, 381 (1967).
215. David R. Webb Co., 291 NLRB 236, 238-240 (1988).
216. Brooks Research & Manufacturing, Inc., 202 NLRB 634, 635-637 (1973).
217. In addition to back wages, a non-reinstated ULP striker may be entitled to pay for vacations, overtime, contributions to welfare, pension, and annuity funds, and reimbursement for out-of-pocket medical expenses incurred during the back pay period. Master Iron Craft Corp., 289 NLRB 1087 (1988).
218. *See, e.g.*, John Morrell & Co. v. South Dakota Dept. of Labor Unemployment Ins. Div., 460 N.W.2d 141, 143-145 (S.D. 1990); In re Sarvis, 251 S.E.2d 434, 437-438 (N.C. 1979).
219. Southwestern Pipe Inc., 179 NLRB 364, 365 (1969) ("A striker may refuse an offer of reinstatement, without losing his status as a striker, because the employer has not made a similar offer to other strikers who are also entitled to immediate reinstatement.").
220. Matlock Truck Body & Trailer Corp., 248 NLRB 461, 463-464 (1980).
221. Lindy's Food Center, 232 NLRB 1001, 1008 (1977). **Note:** If the employer has a legitimate fear of damage from a *surprise* walkout, it may insist that the union agree to provide prior notice of future economic strikes. General Portland Inc., 283 NLRB 826 fn. 2 (1987) (union struck without advance notice and created risk of explosions from flammable gas: when it offered to return, employer insisted that it pledge advance notice of future walkouts).
222. *See* Capehorn Industry, Inc., 336 NLRB 364, 336-337 (2001); Fairfield Tower Condominium Assn., 343 NLRB No. 101 (2004) (one year subcontract).
223. Fairfield Tower Condominium Assn., 343 NLRB No. 101 (2004); Land Air Delivery, Inc., 286 NLRB 1131, 1132 (1987).
224. Central Illinois Public Service Co., 326 NLRB 928 (1998).
225. Eads Transfer, Inc., 304 NLRB 711, 713 (1991) (employer "obligated to declare the lockout before or in immediate response to the strikers' unconditional offers to return to work.").
226. American Ship Bldg. Co. v. NLRB, 380 U.S. 300, 319 (1965) (employer may lock out employees "for the sole purpose of bringing economic pressure to bear in support of his legitimate bargaining position").
227. *See* Clemson Bros. Inc., 290 NLRB 944 (1986).
228. *See* Horsehead Resource Dev. Co., Inc., 321 NLRB 1404, 1404 (1996).
229. R.E. Dietz. Co., 311 NLRB 1259, 1267 (1993) (insistence on nonmandatory subject "converted a lawful lockout, then in existence, into an unlawfully motivated one").
230. Union Terminal Warehouse, Inc. , 286 NLRB 851, 859-861 (1987).
231. Globe Business Furniture, Inc., 290 NLRB 841 fn.2 (1988).
232. Ancor Concepts, Inc., 323 NLRB 742, 744 (1997) ("An employer's use of permanent replacements is inconsistent with a declared lawful lockout in support of its bargaining position."). **Note:** In Johns-Manville Products Corp. v. NLRB,

557 F.2d 1126, 1133 (5th Cir. 1977), the Fifth Circuit Court of Appeals allowed an employer to hire permanent replacements after it locked out employees because of sabotage so severe that it caused the plant to shut down on several occasions. The union's activities were termed an "inside strike." One year later, the Court declined to apply its rule to activities that, while disruptive, did not force a plant to close. NLRB v. Big Three Indus. Gas & Equip. Co., 579 F.2d 304, 313-315 (5th Cir. 1978).

233. Midwest Generation, 343 NLRB No. 12 (2004). **Note:** On October 31, 2005, the Seventh Circuit reversed the Board and ruled that exempting employees from a lockout for the sole reason that they remained at work or returned during a strike is illegal. Local 15, IBEW v. NLRB and Midwest Generation, F.3d (7th Cir. 2005). If this ruling is accepted by the Board, or is adopted by other circuits, it will be more difficult for an employer to declare a lockout when a union offers to return from a strike, as the employer may then have to lay off non-participants and crossovers.

234. Bunting Bearings Corp., 343 NLRB No. 64 (2004).

235. 29 U.S.C §2103(2) ("This chapter shall not apply to a plant closing or mass layoff if....the closing or layoff constitutes a ... lockout not intended to evade the requirements of this chapter."). **Note:** Some state WARN laws, such as California, do not exclude lockouts.

236. International Paper Co., 319 NLRB 1253, 1266-1275 (1995).

237. International Paper Co. v. NLRB, 115 F.3d 1045, 1048-1053 (D.C. Cir. 1997).

238. *See* Movers & Warehousemen's Ass'n., 224 NLRB 356, 357 (1976) ("[A] lockout unlawful at its inception retains its initial taint of illegality until it is terminated and the affected employees are made whole.").

239. *See* Evening News Ass'n, 166 NLRB 219 (1967). There must be a link between the strike and the lockout employers' bargaining positions. *See* David Friedland Painting Co., 158 NLRB 571 (1966) (lockout unlawful because employer sought to intrude in a labor dispute not its own).

240. Ottawa Silica Co., 197 NLRB 449 fn. 2 (1992).

Index

ORDER FORM

Please send me:

_____ copies of *Strikes, Picketing and Inside Campaigns* by Robert M. Schwartz. Price $20.00.

_____ copies of *The Legal Rights of Union Stewards* by Robert M. Schwartz. Price $15.00.

_____ copies of *The FMLA Handbook: A Union Guide to the Family and Medical Leave Act* by Robert M. Schwartz. Price $12.95.

_____ copies of *How to Win Past Practice Grievances* by Robert M. Schwartz. Price $12.95.

_____ copies of *The Labor Law Source Book: Texts of Twenty Federal Labor Laws.* Price $15.00.

Shipping and handling: $4.00 for first book; $2.00 for each additional book, up to maximum of $12.00 for up to 24 books.

For union bulk rates call 1-800-576-4552.

I enclose: $_____

_____

name

_____

address

_____

Fill in and mail with check or money order to Work Rights Press, Box 391066, Cambridge, MA 02139).